Refinance Strategies to Pay Off Your Mortgage Early

How to Use Smart Mortgage Refinancing to Reduce Interest and Accelerate Payoff

By Joseph G. Correa

Copyright & Legal Notice

Published by Live Stronger Faster

First Edition, 2026

Table of Contents

Introduction

For most people, a mortgage is the single largest debt they will ever carry. It often stretches across thirty years, consuming hundreds of thousands of dollars in principal and interest payments over the lifetime of the loan. Many homeowners simply accept this as normal. They make the minimum monthly payment, assume the bank is in control of the timeline, and slowly work toward freedom one payment at a time. Yet what many borrowers fail to realize is that the structure of a mortgage is not fixed in stone. There are strategies available that can dramatically reduce the total interest paid, shorten the life of the loan, improve monthly cash flow, and accelerate the path toward financial freedom. One of the most powerful of these strategies is refinancing.

Refinancing is often misunderstood. Some people view it as something borrowers only do when interest rates fall. Others believe refinancing is only useful for lowering a monthly payment. While those can certainly be valid reasons to refinance, the truth is that refinancing can also become an advanced wealth-building and mortgage payoff strategy when used correctly. A smart refinance can reposition your finances, accelerate your equity growth, reduce years of debt obligations, and help you regain control over your long-term financial future. When combined with intentional planning, disciplined cash flow management, and proper timing, refinancing can become one of the most effective tools available for eliminating mortgage debt faster.

This book was created to help you understand how refinancing truly works and how to use it strategically rather than emotionally. Too many homeowners refinance without a clear objective. They chase lower payments without understanding the long-term costs, extend their mortgage back to thirty years repeatedly, or take cash out without a plan for how the money will improve their financial position. The result is that many borrowers remain trapped in mortgage debt far longer than necessary. This book will show you how to avoid those mistakes and instead use refinancing as a calculated financial tool designed to support your long-term goals.

One of the most important concepts to understand is that refinancing is not inherently good or bad. It is simply a financial instrument. The outcome depends entirely on how it is used. A refinance can either save you enormous amounts of money or quietly increase your debt burden over time. It can shorten your mortgage term and reduce interest costs, or it can reset the clock and keep you paying interest for decades longer. The difference lies in strategy, timing, discipline, and education. That is why learning the mechanics of refinancing is so critical before making any decisions.

Interest rates play a major role in mortgage mathematics. Even a small reduction in your interest rate can save tens or even hundreds of thousands of dollars over the life of a loan. Many homeowners underestimate the power of interest because they only focus on the monthly payment rather than the total cost of borrowing. For example, reducing a mortgage interest rate by just one percent may create enough savings to dramatically shorten the repayment timeline if those savings are applied correctly. This is especially true during the early years of a mortgage when the majority of each payment goes toward interest rather than principal.

Understanding amortization is essential when discussing refinancing strategies. Most traditional mortgages are front-loaded with interest. In the beginning years of a thirty-year loan, borrowers pay a disproportionately high amount toward interest while only a small portion reduces the actual loan balance. Over time, this slowly shifts, allowing more of the payment to go toward principal reduction. Unfortunately, many homeowners refinance multiple times throughout the life of the loan without understanding how restarting the amortization schedule can increase total interest costs. This book will teach you how to refinance without falling into that trap. A refinance done strategically can accelerate amortization rather than restart it negatively. For example, shortening a mortgage from thirty years to fifteen or twenty years can dramatically reduce total interest expenses while building equity at a much faster rate. Some homeowners are surprised to discover that refinancing into a shorter-term loan may not increase the monthly payment as much as expected, especially when combined with lower interest rates. Others may choose hybrid strategies that maintain a manageable payment while making aggressive principal reductions voluntarily. The key is understanding how different refinance structures affect long-term outcomes.

There are several refinance strategies available to homeowners, and each serves a different purpose. Rate-and-term refinancing focuses on improving loan structure by lowering the rate, shortening the term, or both. Cash-out refinancing allows homeowners to access equity for investment opportunities, renovations, debt consolidation, or other financial goals. Streamline refinance programs may provide simplified qualification processes for eligible government-backed loans such as FHA or VA mortgages. Some borrowers refinance to remove mortgage insurance, while others refinance adjustable-rate mortgages into stable fixed-rate structures. Each option has benefits and risks that must be analyzed carefully. One of the biggest mistakes borrowers make is focusing exclusively on monthly payment reduction. While lower payments can improve short-term cash flow, they do not always improve long-term wealth. Extending a mortgage from twenty years back to thirty years may reduce the monthly obligation but substantially increase total interest paid over time. Financial freedom is not just about having a lower payment today. It is about optimizing your overall financial position over decades. This requires balancing payment affordability with long-term debt elimination goals.

This book will encourage you to think differently about mortgage debt. Instead of seeing your mortgage as a passive obligation, you will learn to view it as an active financial system that can be optimized strategically. You will begin evaluating interest rates, loan terms, principal balances, and cash flow decisions through the lens of long-term wealth acceleration. This mindset shift alone can completely transform the way you manage your financial future.

Timing also plays a crucial role in refinancing decisions. Many homeowners wait too long to refinance because they fear closing costs or assume rates will continue dropping indefinitely. Others refinance too quickly without calculating the break-even point or understanding whether the savings justify the costs. Smart refinancing requires careful analysis. You must understand how long you plan to keep the property, how much interest savings you will generate, and whether the refinance aligns with your broader financial objectives. Throughout this book, you will learn how to evaluate refinancing opportunities with clarity and confidence.

Closing costs are another important factor often misunderstood by homeowners. Refinancing is not free. Costs such as lender fees, title charges, appraisal expenses, and prepaid items can impact the overall financial benefit of the transaction. However, focusing only on upfront costs can sometimes prevent borrowers from achieving much larger long-term savings. The true question is not whether refinancing costs money. The real question is whether the refinance creates enough financial improvement to justify the expense. This book will teach you how to analyze refinance costs intelligently instead of emotionally.

Another major advantage of refinancing is flexibility. Mortgage strategies should evolve as your life evolves. Income changes, family responsibilities shift, investment opportunities emerge, and market conditions fluctuate. Refinancing allows borrowers to adapt their mortgage structure to fit changing financial realities. Someone who originally needed a low-payment thirty-year mortgage may later refinance into a shorter-term loan after increasing their income. Another borrower may consolidate high-interest debt into a lower-rate mortgage structure to improve overall financial stability. Refinancing creates options, and options create financial control.

In today's economic environment, financial literacy has become more important than ever. Inflation, rising living costs, fluctuating interest rates, and economic uncertainty have forced many families to rethink how they manage debt and wealth. A mortgage should never operate on autopilot. Homeowners who actively manage their mortgage strategy often place themselves in significantly stronger financial positions than those who simply follow the original repayment schedule without question.

This book is designed for homeowners at many different stages of their financial journey. Whether you recently purchased your first home, have owned property for years, or are approaching retirement, refinance strategies can potentially help improve your financial position. Even borrowers with less-than-perfect situations may discover opportunities to reduce interest costs, restructure debt, or accelerate mortgage payoff timelines. The goal is not perfection. The goal is progress through informed decision-making.

You will also learn that refinancing should never be viewed in isolation. Your mortgage strategy must connect to your broader financial plan. This includes retirement planning, emergency savings, investment goals, business opportunities, tax considerations, and lifestyle priorities. A refinance that appears beneficial on paper may not align with your overall wealth strategy if it weakens liquidity or creates unnecessary risk. Likewise, a refinance that slightly increases monthly payments may dramatically strengthen long-term financial security by eliminating years of interest costs. Context matters.

As you move through this book, you will discover practical examples, real-world strategies, and advanced concepts designed to help you think critically about mortgage optimization. You will learn how interest savings compound over time, how shorter loan terms accelerate equity growth, how principal reductions change amortization dynamics, and how refinancing can either strengthen or weaken your path to financial independence depending on how it is structured.

You will also begin to recognize that financial freedom is rarely achieved through one massive decision alone. Instead, it is often the result of many smaller intelligent decisions made consistently over time. Refinancing can become one of those critical decisions that changes the trajectory of your finances permanently. A well-structured refinance can create momentum that accelerates debt elimination, improves cash flow management, and opens the door to greater financial opportunities in the future. Most importantly, this book aims to empower you with knowledge. Mortgage lenders, banks, and financial institutions have access to sophisticated information and tools that many consumers never fully understand. When borrowers lack financial education, they often rely entirely on others to guide major decisions involving hundreds of thousands of dollars. This book is designed to help close that gap. The more you understand refinancing, amortization, interest structures, and mortgage strategy, the more confidently you can make decisions that benefit your future rather than simply benefiting the lender.

Your mortgage does not have to control your life for thirty years. With the right knowledge, planning, and execution, you can take ownership of the repayment process and potentially eliminate debt years earlier than expected. Refinancing is not merely about changing a loan. It is about changing the direction of your financial future. It is about creating leverage, improving efficiency, and accelerating progress toward freedom.

Welcome to Refinance Strategies to Pay Off Your Mortgage Early. This book will help you understand how to use smart mortgage refinancing techniques to reduce interest, optimize cash flow, accelerate equity growth, and move closer to long-term financial independence. The journey toward mortgage freedom begins with education, strategy, and the willingness to think differently about debt, wealth, and opportunity.

Chapter 1

Understanding How Mortgage Refinancing Really Works

Most homeowners hear the word "refinancing" throughout their lives, yet very few truly understand what it means or how powerful it can become when used strategically. Many borrowers assume refinancing is simply replacing one mortgage with another to get a lower payment. While that can certainly be one outcome, refinancing is much more than that. At its core, refinancing is the process of restructuring your mortgage debt to improve your financial position. This restructuring can reduce interest costs, shorten repayment timelines, improve monthly cash flow, eliminate mortgage insurance, consolidate debt, access equity, or reposition a homeowner for long-term wealth acceleration.

To understand refinancing correctly, you must first understand how a mortgage functions over time. A mortgage is not simply a fixed monthly payment. It is a highly structured financial instrument built around interest calculations, amortization schedules, risk analysis, and long-term repayment systems. The bank earns money primarily through interest. During the early years of a traditional mortgage, a very large portion of your payment goes toward interest rather than principal reduction. This is one of the reasons why homeowners often feel frustrated after making payments for years while seeing only modest decreases in their loan balance.

For example, someone with a thirty-year mortgage may discover that after five years of payments, the principal balance has not declined nearly as much as expected. This happens because mortgages are amortized. Amortization refers to the way payments are structured over time. In the beginning years, the lender collects more interest because the loan balance is still high. As the balance gradually decreases, the amount of interest charged each month slowly declines, allowing more of the payment to reduce principal. This system heavily favors lenders during the early stages of the mortgage.

Understanding amortization is critical because refinancing resets the mortgage structure. When a borrower refinances, the old loan is paid off and replaced with a new one. The terms of the new loan may differ significantly from the original mortgage. The interest rate may change. The loan term may become shorter or longer. The payment structure may shift from adjustable to fixed or vice versa. The borrower may also choose to take cash out from accumulated equity. Each of these changes impacts the long-term cost of the mortgage. One of the most common reasons homeowners refinance is to obtain a lower interest rate. Even a small reduction in rate can create substantial savings over the life of the loan. Interest rates directly affect the amount of money borrowers pay to lenders over time. A lower rate means less interest accrues monthly, which can reduce both the monthly payment and the total long-term borrowing cost. However, lower payments alone should never be the only factor considered when evaluating a refinance opportunity.

Many borrowers become trapped by focusing solely on short-term monthly savings while ignoring the long-term implications of resetting the loan term. Imagine a homeowner who has already paid on a thirty-year mortgage for ten years. If that borrower refinances into a brand-new thirty-year mortgage, they may reduce the payment temporarily, but they also restart the amortization process. This means they may spend another thirty years paying interest unless additional strategies are implemented. In some cases, borrowers unknowingly extend their mortgage debt far beyond their original repayment timeline simply because they chased lower monthly payments repeatedly.

This does not mean refinancing is bad. It simply means refinancing must be approached strategically. A refinance should always serve a specific purpose tied to long-term financial goals. Sometimes lowering the payment is appropriate, especially if improving cash flow helps avoid financial stress or frees up money for investments, business growth, or emergency savings. Other times, a borrower may benefit more from shortening the loan term and aggressively accelerating payoff rather than minimizing the payment.

One of the most powerful refinance strategies involves transitioning from a thirty-year mortgage into a shorter-term loan such as a twenty-year, fifteen-year, or even ten-year mortgage. Shorter loan terms generally carry lower interest rates because lenders face less long-term risk. In addition, shorter terms accelerate principal reduction dramatically. This means borrowers build equity faster while paying substantially less interest overall. Although monthly payments may increase, the long-term financial benefits can be enormous.

Consider a homeowner who originally borrowed $400,000 on a thirty-year mortgage at a higher interest rate. After several years of payments and some appreciation in property value, they refinance into a fifteen-year loan with a significantly lower rate. Their monthly payment may rise moderately, but the amount of interest saved over the life of the loan could potentially reach hundreds of thousands of dollars. More importantly, the borrower could eliminate mortgage debt decades earlier, dramatically improving long-term financial freedom. Refinancing also becomes powerful when combined with disciplined principal reduction strategies. Some homeowners refinance into lower-rate loans but continue making payments equal to the previous higher payment amount. The difference between the old payment and the new required payment is applied directly toward principal reduction. This strategy can accelerate payoff timelines aggressively without forcing borrowers into excessively short loan terms. It combines flexibility with accelerated debt elimination.

Another important refinance strategy involves removing mortgage insurance. Many borrowers who purchase homes with smaller down payments are required to pay private mortgage insurance, commonly called PMI. FHA loans may include mortgage insurance premiums as well. These insurance costs can add hundreds of dollars per month to the mortgage payment without reducing the actual loan balance. As property values rise and principal balances decline, borrowers may become eligible to refinance into conventional loans without mortgage insurance requirements. Eliminating these extra costs can significantly improve cash flow and accelerate wealth accumulation.

Cash-out refinancing is another area that requires careful understanding. A cash-out refinance allows homeowners to borrow against the equity built in their property. The old mortgage is replaced with a larger loan, and the borrower receives the difference in cash. This strategy can be extremely dangerous when used irresponsibly, but it can also become a powerful financial tool when used intelligently. Some homeowners use cash-out refinances to consolidate high-interest debt, renovate properties, invest in businesses, purchase rental properties, or create additional income streams.

The key issue is whether the borrowed funds create financial improvement or financial destruction. Borrowing equity to fund consumer spending, luxury purchases, or depreciating assets often weakens long-term financial stability. In contrast, using equity strategically to acquire appreciating or income-producing assets may strengthen wealth-building potential. This distinction is critical. Debt itself is not inherently good or bad. The purpose behind the debt determines whether it improves or damages your financial future.

Market conditions also influence refinancing opportunities. Interest rates fluctuate constantly based on inflation, economic policy, bond markets, employment trends, and broader financial conditions. Homeowners who monitor rates strategically may identify opportunities to refinance during favorable market cycles. However, timing the market perfectly is nearly impossible. Instead of obsessing over finding the absolute lowest rate possible, borrowers should focus on whether the refinance meaningfully improves their financial position compared to their current mortgage structure.

Closing costs are another factor borrowers must evaluate carefully. Refinancing involves fees such as lender charges, title costs, appraisal fees, recording fees, and prepaid escrow expenses. Some homeowners become discouraged by these costs and avoid refinancing altogether. However, the true evaluation should involve calculating the break-even point. This refers to the amount of time required for monthly savings to exceed the upfront refinance costs. If a refinance saves $300 per month and costs $6,000, the break-even period would be approximately twenty months. If the borrower plans to stay in the property much longer than that, the refinance may still create significant long-term value.

Credit scores and financial positioning also affect refinance opportunities. Borrowers with stronger credit profiles generally qualify for better interest rates and loan terms. Debt-to-income ratios, employment stability, equity levels, and cash reserves also influence lender decisions. Improving financial health before refinancing can sometimes produce dramatically better results. Paying down debt, increasing savings, correcting credit report errors, or waiting for appreciation to improve loan-to-value ratios may strengthen refinance options significantly. Home equity plays a central role in refinance decisions. Equity represents the portion of the property the homeowner truly owns. As mortgage balances decline and property values increase, equity grows. Higher equity levels often improve refinance eligibility while reducing lender risk. Some refinance programs require minimum equity thresholds, especially for cash-out transactions. Understanding how equity impacts financing options is critical for long-term mortgage planning.

Refinancing can also create psychological benefits beyond pure mathematics. Many homeowners experience reduced stress and increased confidence after restructuring their mortgage strategically. Knowing that you are actively reducing interest costs, accelerating payoff timelines, or improving financial efficiency creates momentum and motivation. Financial progress often encourages stronger money habits overall, including budgeting, investing, and long-term planning.

One of the biggest mindset shifts homeowners must make is recognizing that mortgage management is not passive. Too many borrowers obtain a mortgage and then simply make payments for decades without reevaluating their strategy. Wealthier and more financially educated individuals tend to manage debt actively. They monitor interest rates, evaluate refinance opportunities, optimize cash flow, and reposition liabilities strategically as conditions change. This active approach can create substantial long-term advantages.

Refinancing should never be based purely on emotion or fear. Some borrowers panic during rising rate environments and rush into poor decisions. Others refuse to refinance out of fear of paperwork or mistrust of lenders, even when enormous savings opportunities exist. Emotional decision-making often creates costly financial outcomes. Smart refinancing requires analysis, patience, discipline, and a clear understanding of long-term goals.

As you continue through this book, you will learn advanced refinance concepts designed to help you evaluate opportunities intelligently. You will discover how loan terms affect interest costs, how amortization impacts long-term wealth, how refinancing interacts with broader investment strategies, and how to avoid common mistakes that keep homeowners trapped in debt longer than necessary. Most importantly, you will begin viewing refinancing not as a random financial event but as a strategic system that can accelerate financial independence when used correctly.

Mortgage debt does not have to last thirty years. With the right strategy, many homeowners can eliminate years or even decades from their repayment timeline while simultaneously improving cash flow and building wealth. Refinancing is one of the most powerful tools available for accomplishing this goal. The key is understanding how it works, why it works, and when to use it.

The journey toward mortgage freedom begins with education. Once you understand the mechanics behind refinancing, you gain the ability to make decisions with confidence rather than confusion. You begin seeing opportunities where others only see monthly payments. You recognize that every interest rate, loan term, and principal reduction decision shapes your future. This awareness creates power, and financial power creates options. The more options you have, the more control you gain over your financial destiny.

The Refinance Decision That Changed Everything

Michael and Elena never imagined that a single financial decision could completely transform their future. For years, they lived the way most middle-class families do. They worked hard, paid their bills on time, raised two children, and tried to save what little they could after monthly expenses. They purchased their first home in their early thirties using a thirty-year fixed mortgage. At the time, they were simply grateful to become homeowners. They believed that making their monthly payment consistently meant they were building wealth automatically.

For the first several years, they rarely thought about the mortgage itself. The payment came out every month, and life continued moving forward. Michael worked long hours managing operations for a distribution company while Elena worked as a school administrator. Their incomes slowly increased over time, but so did their expenses. Their children became involved in sports, extracurricular activities, and private tutoring programs. Insurance premiums rose. Groceries became more expensive. Property taxes increased steadily every year.

Although they earned decent incomes, they constantly felt financially stretched. The mortgage payment remained their largest monthly expense, and despite making payments for nearly eight years, the loan balance still seemed frustratingly high. Michael occasionally checked the mortgage statements and felt discouraged seeing how much of each payment still went toward interest.

One evening, while reviewing their finances at the kitchen table, Elena asked a simple question that would eventually change everything.

“How much longer do we still have on this mortgage?”

Michael opened the online account and stared at the screen.

"Twenty-two years," he replied quietly. The number felt overwhelming. Twenty-two more years of payments. Twenty-two more years tied to the bank. Twenty-two more years before true ownership and financial flexibility.

That realization stayed with them for weeks.

Around the same time, interest rates in the market had started falling. Michael began hearing coworkers discuss refinancing. Some talked about lowering their monthly payments. Others mentioned pulling cash out for renovations or debt consolidation. At first, Michael dismissed the idea. He assumed refinancing would be complicated, expensive, or risky. He also worried about restarting the loan clock and being trapped for even longer.

Still, curiosity pushed him to research further.

The more he learned, the more he realized most homeowners misunderstood refinancing entirely. He discovered that refinancing was not just about lowering payments. It could also be used strategically to shorten the mortgage term, reduce interest dramatically, and accelerate financial freedom. He began running mortgage calculations late at night after the children went to sleep.

One scenario caught his attention immediately.

If they refinanced from their current thirty-year mortgage into a fifteen-year loan at a significantly lower interest rate, their payment would increase, but not by nearly as much as they expected. More importantly, the total interest savings over time would be enormous.

Michael printed the amortization comparisons and showed them to Elena the next morning.

"If we stay with our current loan," he explained, "we'll keep paying for another twenty-two years and spend a huge amount in interest."

Elena looked at the numbers carefully.

"And if we refinance?"

"We could potentially pay off the house in fifteen years or less."

The idea felt impossible at first. Fifteen years sounded aggressive compared to what they were used to. Yet as they reviewed their budget more carefully, they realized something important. Over the years, their incomes had increased substantially, but their financial habits had expanded with their earnings. Dining out had become more frequent. Subscription services accumulated silently. Vacations became more expensive. Small lifestyle upgrades slowly consumed the extra income they once thought would improve their finances permanently. For the first time, they began questioning whether short-term comfort was costing them long-term freedom.

After weeks of discussions, they decided to move forward with the refinance.

The process required gathering income documentation, tax returns, bank statements, and credit information. At times it felt stressful, but they remained focused on the bigger picture. When the refinance closed, they officially replaced their remaining twenty-two-year mortgage timeline with a new fifteen-year strategy at a significantly lower interest rate.

The first few months felt uncomfortable. Their payment increased enough that they had to become more disciplined with spending. They reduced unnecessary subscriptions, cut back on impulsive purchases, and created a more intentional monthly budget. Surprisingly, instead of feeling restricted, they began feeling empowered.

For the first time in years, they felt like they were actively controlling their future instead of simply reacting to bills.

As time passed, the results became increasingly motivating.

Because the new mortgage carried a lower interest rate and shorter amortization schedule, a much larger percentage of every payment reduced principal immediately. The balance started dropping noticeably. Unlike their previous mortgage, where progress felt painfully slow, they now saw meaningful reductions every single month.

Michael became obsessed with tracking the numbers. He checked the amortization schedule regularly and calculated how much additional interest they were saving with every extra principal payment they made. Elena began redirecting bonuses and tax refunds toward the mortgage instead of spending them automatically.

Then something unexpected happened.

As their mortgage balance declined faster, they felt less financial anxiety overall. The pressure that once controlled their decisions slowly began disappearing. They started building larger emergency reserves. They invested more consistently into retirement accounts. Their confidence increased because they knew their largest debt was shrinking rapidly.

Five years into the refinance strategy, Michael received a promotion that significantly increased his income. Instead of expanding their lifestyle dramatically, they applied most of the additional income toward principal reduction. Every extra payment shortened the mortgage timeline even further.

Friends and family often questioned why they were so focused on paying down the house aggressively.

"You could invest that money instead," some said.

"You should enjoy life more," others argued.

Michael and Elena understood the comments, but they also understood something deeper. They were not just paying off a mortgage. They were purchasing freedom.

As the years passed, the transformation became undeniable. Their mortgage balance dropped faster and faster. Interest charges became smaller each month. Financial flexibility expanded. They no longer feared job instability or economic downturns the way they once had.

Then came the day they never thought would arrive so quickly.

The mortgage was gone.

Years earlier, they had expected to remain in debt well into their fifties. Instead, through one strategic refinance decision combined with discipline and consistency, they eliminated their mortgage years ahead of schedule.

The emotional impact surprised them more than anything else.

Michael sat quietly in the living room after making the final payment confirmation online. Elena walked in holding coffee, and both simply stared at each other for a moment.

"No more mortgage," she whispered.

For the first time in decades, the house truly belonged to them.

No lender. No monthly obligation. No interest payments draining their future.

That financial freedom changed every aspect of their lives. They invested more aggressively. They traveled without financial stress. They helped their children with college expenses without sacrificing retirement security. Most importantly, they gained peace of mind that no market fluctuation or economic headline could easily take away.

Looking back, Michael realized the refinance itself was not the true turning point. The real transformation happened when they stopped viewing their mortgage as a passive monthly bill and started treating it like a financial system that could be optimized strategically.

That shift in thinking changed everything.

And for millions of homeowners willing to educate themselves and take action, the same opportunity exists.

Chapter 2

Lowering Your Interest Rate to Accelerate Mortgage Payoff

One of the most powerful financial advantages available to homeowners is the ability to lower the interest rate on their mortgage through refinancing. While many borrowers focus primarily on monthly payment reductions, the true power of a lower interest rate extends far beyond short-term affordability. A reduced interest rate changes the mathematical structure of the loan itself. It alters how quickly interest accumulates, how efficiently principal is reduced, and how rapidly financial freedom can be achieved. Understanding how interest rates impact long-term mortgage costs is essential for anyone seeking to pay off their home faster while building long-term wealth.

Interest is the price borrowers pay for the privilege of using borrowed money. Every mortgage payment contains two primary components: principal and interest. Principal reduces the actual loan balance, while interest compensates the lender for the loan. In the early years of most mortgages, interest consumes a substantial portion of the payment. This is why so many homeowners feel frustrated after making payments for years while seeing relatively little progress in reducing their balance. The interest rate attached to a mortgage determines how aggressively interest accumulates over time. Even small differences in rates can produce enormous changes in total repayment costs. Many homeowners underestimate this because they focus only on the monthly payment rather than examining the total amount paid over the life of the loan. However, mortgage mathematics operate over decades, not months. A seemingly minor rate reduction may create tens or hundreds of thousands of dollars in long-term savings.

For example, imagine two homeowners borrowing the same amount for the same property. One secures a mortgage at a significantly higher interest rate, while the other obtains a lower rate through refinancing or better timing. Over thirty years, the borrower with the lower rate may save enough money to fully fund retirement investments, purchase additional properties, or eliminate years of debt payments entirely. The difference is not just numerical. It represents years of financial freedom, reduced stress, and expanded opportunity.

Lowering your interest rate reduces the amount of interest charged monthly on the remaining loan balance. This means more of each payment goes directly toward principal reduction. Once principal decreases faster, the mortgage balance begins shrinking more aggressively. This creates momentum. As the balance declines, future interest charges decrease further because interest is calculated on a smaller amount. Over time, this compounding effect accelerates the payoff process dramatically.

One of the biggest misconceptions about refinancing is the belief that lowering the monthly payment automatically means the borrower is making financial progress. While lower payments can certainly help improve cash flow, true progress depends on how the savings are used. If a homeowner refinances into a lower-rate loan but spends all the monthly savings on lifestyle upgrades or unnecessary expenses, the refinance may create little long-term improvement. However, if the borrower redirects the savings toward additional principal payments, investments, emergency reserves, or other wealth-building strategies, the refinance becomes transformational.

This is why intentionality matters so much in refinance planning. A lower interest rate creates opportunity, but opportunity alone does not guarantee financial improvement. The borrower's decisions determine the outcome. Some homeowners use lower rates to free themselves from debt faster. Others unintentionally use lower rates to expand spending habits while remaining trapped in long-term financial obligations. The refinance itself is simply a tool.

Discipline determines whether the tool creates freedom or merely temporary relief. Timing plays a major role in interest rate strategy. Mortgage rates fluctuate continuously based on inflation, Federal Reserve policies, bond markets, employment data, economic growth expectations, and broader financial conditions. Homeowners who monitor market conditions carefully may identify opportunities to refinance during favorable cycles. However, waiting indefinitely for the "perfect" rate can become dangerous. Many borrowers spend years hesitating, hoping rates will drop slightly further, only to miss opportunities entirely when rates begin rising again.

The goal should not necessarily be obtaining the absolute lowest rate possible. Instead, the focus should be on whether refinancing meaningfully improves the borrower's financial position compared to the existing loan structure. A refinance that lowers the rate enough to produce substantial savings may still be valuable even if rates later decline slightly more. Financial progress often comes from taking intelligent action consistently rather than attempting to achieve perfection.

Shortening the loan term while lowering the rate can create even greater financial acceleration. For example, a homeowner may refinance from a thirty-year mortgage into a fifteen-year mortgage at a lower interest rate. Although the monthly payment may increase, the amount of interest saved can be extraordinary. This occurs because shorter-term loans reduce both the interest rate and the number of years interest accumulates. The combination creates a powerful debt elimination strategy.

Many borrowers initially fear shorter loan terms because they focus only on the higher payment. However, they often fail to consider how much financial energy is wasted paying interest for decades longer than necessary. Every extra year of mortgage debt represents additional interest flowing to the lender rather than remaining in the borrower's control. Eliminating those years can dramatically improve long-term wealth potential.

Another powerful strategy involves maintaining the same payment amount after refinancing into a lower-rate loan. Suppose a homeowner currently pays $3,000 monthly on a higher-rate mortgage. After refinancing into a lower-rate loan, the required payment drops to $2,500. Instead of reducing their actual payment, the homeowner continues paying $3,000 monthly. The extra $500 goes directly toward principal reduction. This approach allows the borrower to accelerate payoff aggressively without feeling a major lifestyle change because they were already accustomed to making the higher payment.

This strategy becomes especially effective when combined with periodic lump-sum payments from bonuses, commissions, side income, tax refunds, or business profits. Over time, the accelerated principal reduction compounds dramatically. The homeowner reduces interest costs further because every additional principal payment lowers future interest calculations immediately.

Homeowners must also understand the relationship between inflation and interest rates. Inflation affects purchasing power over time, and lenders adjust rates partly based on inflation expectations. During low-rate environments, borrowers may have opportunities to secure historically favorable financing terms. Fixed-rate mortgages become especially valuable because they lock in predictable payments for decades while inflation may continue raising wages, rents, and living costs over time.

A lower fixed interest rate creates financial stability. Homeowners know exactly what their principal and interest payment will remain throughout the loan term. This predictability allows for more accurate long-term financial planning. In contrast, adjustable-rate mortgages may introduce uncertainty because rates and payments can change over time. While adjustable loans may initially offer lower rates, borrowers must understand the potential risks associated with future payment increases.

Credit quality also plays a significant role in securing lower rates. Borrowers with strong credit profiles typically qualify for the best financing terms available. This means improving your credit score before refinancing may significantly increase long-term savings. Paying bills consistently, reducing credit card balances, avoiding unnecessary debt, and correcting inaccuracies on credit reports can strengthen refinance opportunities substantially.

Loan-to-value ratio also impacts refinance pricing. Homeowners with higher equity levels generally qualify for better rates because lenders face less risk. As property values appreciate and balances decline, refinancing opportunities may improve naturally. This is one reason why maintaining home value and making extra principal payments can strengthen future mortgage strategies.

Closing costs must always be evaluated carefully when pursuing lower interest rates. Refinancing is not free. Borrowers often pay lender fees, title charges, appraisal expenses, escrow adjustments, and other costs. However, many homeowners focus too heavily on upfront expenses while ignoring long-term savings. The key calculation involves determining the break-even point and evaluating total interest savings over time.

For example, if refinancing costs $5,000 but reduces monthly payments by $400, the break-even period would be approximately thirteen months. After that point, the borrower begins generating net savings. Over many years, the cumulative savings may become extremely significant. Understanding these calculations allows borrowers to make informed decisions rather than emotional ones.

Psychology also plays an important role in mortgage management. Lower interest rates often create emotional relief because homeowners feel more financially efficient and secure. This increased confidence can motivate stronger money habits overall. Some borrowers begin budgeting more intentionally, investing consistently, or paying down other debts more aggressively after successfully refinancing.

One overlooked benefit of lowering interest rates is increased financial flexibility. When less money flows toward interest each month, homeowners gain greater control over their cash flow. They may redirect savings toward retirement accounts, emergency funds, business investments, rental properties, or educational opportunities. This flexibility creates options, and financial options are one of the foundations of long-term wealth.

Lower interest rates can also provide protection during economic uncertainty. Families with lower debt costs generally experience less financial stress during recessions, job disruptions, or unexpected emergencies. Reduced obligations create breathing room that may help homeowners avoid financial crises that could otherwise become overwhelming.

Many financially successful individuals understand that managing debt intelligently is often more important than simply avoiding debt entirely. The goal is not necessarily to eliminate all debt immediately at any cost. The goal is to optimize debt structures so that money flows efficiently toward long-term financial goals. Lowering mortgage interest rates is one of the most effective ways to improve that efficiency.

Throughout history, homeowners who actively managed their mortgages strategically often positioned themselves far ahead financially compared to those who passively accepted their original loan terms forever. Markets change. Rates change. Financial circumstances change. Mortgage strategies should evolve accordingly. Refinancing allows borrowers to adapt their financial structure to changing opportunities and goals.

Ultimately, lowering your interest rate is not merely about saving money each month. It is about reclaiming financial power over time. Every dollar not wasted on unnecessary interest becomes a dollar that can build wealth, create security, expand opportunities, and accelerate freedom. Over decades, these differences become life-changing. A mortgage can either become a financial burden that limits your future or a financial system that supports long-term wealth creation. Lowering your interest rate is one of the most important steps toward transforming your mortgage from a passive liability into an active financial advantage. The homeowners who understand this principle place themselves in stronger positions not only to eliminate debt faster but also to build lasting financial independence.

The Interest Rate That Changed Their Future

When Carlos and Sophia purchased their home, they felt proud simply to qualify for the mortgage. They were both in their early thirties, recently married, and excited to finally stop renting. After years of saving, they purchased a modest home in a growing neighborhood just outside the city.

At the time, mortgage rates were higher than they had hoped, but they convinced themselves it was still worth it. Their loan officer assured them they could always refinance later if rates improved. Carlos barely understood what refinancing meant, and Sophia focused more on whether the monthly payment fit their budget. Like most first-time buyers, they were overwhelmed by paperwork, inspections, escrow calculations, and closing disclosures. Once they received the keys, they simply moved forward with life. For the first few years, the mortgage payment consumed a huge portion of their income. Carlos worked in commercial HVAC sales while Sophia managed a dental office. They earned enough to stay afloat comfortably, but there was never much extra. Vacations were limited. Savings grew slowly. Unexpected expenses often disrupted their plans.

Every month, they made the mortgage payment automatically without thinking much about it. Occasionally Carlos checked the loan balance online and felt disappointed by how little progress they seemed to be making.

"We've paid for four years already," he said one night while reviewing their account. "How is the balance still this high?"

Sophia looked over his shoulder.

"It feels like we're barely moving."

What they didn't fully understand was how heavily their mortgage payments were weighted toward interest during the early years. Most of their money was going to the lender rather than reducing principal.

Then the economy shifted.

Interest rates began dropping significantly. Friends started talking about refinancing constantly. Some bragged about lowering their payments. Others used refinances to pay off credit cards or renovate kitchens. Carlos initially ignored the conversations. He assumed refinancing was complicated and expensive. Besides, life was busy. Their first child had recently been born, daycare costs were increasing, and work responsibilities consumed most of his attention.

One evening, however, Sophia showed him an online mortgage calculator.

"Look at this," she said.

Carlos stared at the numbers silently.

The calculator compared their current mortgage with a potential refinance at a much lower interest rate. The difference shocked him. Not only could they lower their payment, but they could also save an enormous amount in long-term interest.

"That can't be right," he said.

But it was.

For the first time, Carlos began understanding how much interest rates affected total borrowing costs. He realized they were on track to pay hundreds of thousands of dollars in interest over the life of the loan if they changed nothing.

The next weekend, they met with a mortgage professional to explore refinance options. At first, they assumed the best strategy would simply involve lowering the monthly payment as much as possible. However, during the conversation, the mortgage advisor introduced another idea.

“What if instead of restarting another thirty-year loan,” he explained, “you refinanced into a shorter term?”

Carlos hesitated immediately.

“Aren’t fifteen-year mortgages way more expensive monthly?”

“Not always as much as people think,” the advisor replied.

They reviewed the numbers carefully.

Because interest rates had fallen so significantly, the payment difference between their current mortgage and a shorter-term refinance was smaller than expected. More importantly, the amount of long-term interest savings was enormous.

Sophia looked at Carlos carefully.

"If we can make this work," she said quietly, "we could own this house so much sooner."

The idea stayed with them for days.

At home, they reviewed every area of their spending. They realized they had slowly increased lifestyle expenses over the years without noticing. Multiple streaming services, expensive dining habits, impulse shopping, upgraded vehicles, and unnecessary subscriptions quietly consumed large amounts of income.

None of it individually seemed extreme, but together it prevented meaningful financial progress.

After several discussions, they made the decision to refinance into a shorter-term loan at a much lower interest rate.

The refinance process required discipline. They gathered tax returns, pay stubs, bank statements, and employment records. There were moments of stress and uncertainty, but when the refinance finally closed, everything changed.

For the first time, they felt like they had a real plan.

Their payment increased moderately, but because the interest rate was dramatically lower, far more of each payment reduced principal immediately. Carlos became fascinated watching the balance decline faster than ever before.

Every month, they reviewed the amortization schedule together.

"This is unbelievable," Sophia said one evening. "We're making more progress in one year than we used to make in three."

The psychological effect was powerful.

Instead of feeling trapped by the mortgage, they felt empowered by it. Every payment now felt productive instead of discouraging.

As their incomes increased over time, they avoided the temptation to inflate their lifestyle dramatically. Instead, they applied bonuses and raises toward principal reduction. Whenever Carlos earned extra commissions, they sent additional payments directly to the loan balance.

Friends questioned their decisions constantly.

"Why not enjoy the money now?"

"Why are you so aggressive paying off the house?"

But Carlos and Sophia understood something most people overlooked. Lowering the interest rate was not just about the house. It was about reclaiming years of their lives financially.

The lower rate created momentum. The shorter term created urgency. Together, they transformed the entire trajectory of their future.

Five years after refinancing, they had already reduced the mortgage balance far beyond what they originally believed possible. More importantly, their confidence grew with every passing year. They built larger investment accounts. They expanded emergency savings. Financial stress declined dramatically.

Then came a moment neither of them expected.

Sophia decided to leave her demanding management position and start a small pediatric dental consulting business from home. Years earlier, this would have felt financially impossible. But because their mortgage balance had fallen so aggressively and their overall financial position had strengthened, they had flexibility.

The lower interest rate had not only saved them money. It had created options.

Years later, when they finally paid off the mortgage completely, Carlos sat quietly on the back patio looking across the yard they once worried they could barely afford.

Sophia walked outside holding the mortgage payoff letter.

"No more payments," she whispered.

Carlos smiled slowly.

"All because we stopped treating the mortgage like something permanent." The refinance decision had done far more than reduce interest. It had changed the way they thought about money, debt, freedom, and time itself.

And once that mindset changed, everything else followed.

Chapter 3

Choosing the Right Loan Term to Eliminate Your Mortgage Faster

One of the most important decisions homeowners make when refinancing is choosing the loan term. While many borrowers focus almost entirely on securing the lowest possible interest rate, the length of the loan itself often has an even greater impact on long-term financial outcomes. The loan term determines how long interest accumulates, how quickly principal is reduced, how aggressively equity grows, and how rapidly financial freedom can be achieved. Understanding how loan terms work is essential for homeowners who want to eliminate mortgage debt strategically rather than simply making payments indefinitely.

A loan term refers to the amount of time scheduled for repayment of the mortgage. The most common mortgage structure in the United States is the thirty-year fixed-rate loan. This loan became popular because it creates relatively affordable monthly payments by spreading repayment over a long period of time. While this improves accessibility for homebuyers, it also dramatically increases the total amount of interest paid over the life of the loan. Many homeowners never stop to calculate the true long-term cost of extending mortgage debt across thirty years. A thirty-year loan may appear manageable monthly, but the lender collects interest for decades. The borrower sacrifices enormous amounts of money over time simply because repayment is stretched so far into the future. This is why understanding the relationship between loan term and total interest cost is so important.

Shorter loan terms function differently. Fifteen-year, twenty-year, and even ten-year mortgages accelerate principal repayment substantially. Because the balance declines more rapidly, interest accumulates over fewer years and on smaller balances. The result is dramatically lower total interest costs and much faster equity growth. Although monthly payments are higher, the long-term financial benefits can be life-changing.

Many borrowers initially reject shorter loan terms because they focus only on the increased monthly obligation. However, this perspective often ignores the enormous financial advantages gained over time. A higher payment is not necessarily negative if it dramatically reduces total debt costs and accelerates freedom. The real question is not simply whether the payment is higher. The question is whether the payment aligns with the borrower's long-term goals and financial capacity.

For example, imagine two homeowners borrowing the same amount at similar interest rates. One chooses a thirty-year mortgage while the other chooses a fifteen-year mortgage. The borrower with the fifteen-year loan may pay substantially more monthly, but they eliminate the debt in half the time and save enormous amounts in interest. In many cases, the total interest savings alone can equal hundreds of thousands of dollars depending on the loan size and interest rate environment.

The emotional impact of shorter loan terms is often underestimated as well. Homeowners carrying mortgage debt for decades frequently experience ongoing financial pressure. The mortgage becomes a permanent background obligation influencing every financial decision. In contrast, borrowers aggressively pursuing shorter payoff timelines often feel empowered, focused, and motivated because they can see tangible progress toward complete ownership and financial independence.

Refinancing creates an opportunity to reevaluate your mortgage strategy entirely. Many homeowners begin with thirty-year mortgages because they need lower payments initially. However, years later, their financial situation may improve significantly. Income increases, debts decrease, careers stabilize, and financial priorities evolve. What once felt necessary may no longer be optimal. Refinancing into a shorter-term loan can reposition homeowners to capitalize on improved financial circumstances. One of the most common refinance strategies involves transitioning from a thirty-year mortgage into a twenty-year or fifteen-year loan after several years of income growth. Because the borrower has already reduced some principal and potentially benefits from lower interest rates, the payment increase may be far more manageable than expected. In some cases, borrowers are surprised to discover they can accelerate payoff dramatically with only a moderate monthly increase.

Another strategy involves refinancing into a shorter-term loan while continuing to make additional principal payments voluntarily. This hybrid approach creates flexibility. The borrower commits to a more aggressive repayment schedule but still maintains the ability to accelerate even further when cash flow permits. Bonuses, commissions, side income, or tax refunds can all be applied strategically toward principal reduction.

Some homeowners fear shorter loan terms because they worry about losing financial flexibility. This concern is understandable. Higher required payments reduce short-term discretionary cash flow. However, many borrowers overlook the fact that carrying mortgage debt for decades also reduces flexibility. Long-term debt obligations limit investment options, delay retirement planning, increase stress during economic uncertainty, and expose borrowers to prolonged financial risk.

The key is balance. Choosing the right loan term requires evaluating income stability, emergency reserves, lifestyle priorities, investment goals, family responsibilities, and long-term objectives. There is no universal perfect loan term for every person. The ideal structure depends on the borrower's unique financial situation and desired timeline for freedom.

Twenty-year mortgages often provide a middle ground between aggressive payoff and manageable payments. They reduce interest significantly compared to thirty-year loans while keeping payments lower than fifteen-year structures. Some borrowers prefer twenty-year terms because they accelerate progress without creating excessive financial pressure. Others choose fifteen-year loans specifically because the shorter timeline forces stronger financial discipline and creates faster momentum.

Ten-year mortgages represent an even more aggressive approach. These loans carry very high monthly payments but eliminate debt rapidly while minimizing interest dramatically.

They are often used by high-income earners, late-stage homeowners, or individuals approaching retirement who prioritize eliminating debt quickly. While not appropriate for everyone, ten-year structures can create extraordinary long-term financial efficiency for borrowers with stable cash flow and strong financial reserves. One critical concept borrowers must understand is that loan terms directly affect amortization speed. On longer loans, principal reduction occurs slowly because payments are spread over more years. On shorter loans, principal declines aggressively almost immediately. This accelerated amortization changes the entire financial dynamic of the mortgage.

For example, on a traditional thirty-year loan, borrowers may spend years watching balances decline painfully slowly because interest dominates the payments initially. In contrast, shorter-term loans allocate much larger portions of each payment toward principal from the very beginning. This creates visible progress quickly, which often motivates homeowners to remain committed to their payoff strategy.

Another important factor involves total lifetime cash flow. Many homeowners focus only on monthly affordability without recognizing how much long-term income will eventually be consumed by interest. Every dollar paid in unnecessary interest represents money that cannot be invested, saved, donated, or used to improve quality of life. Choosing a shorter loan term allows more future income to remain under the borrower's control rather than flowing to lenders.

Mortgage freedom also affects retirement planning significantly. Homeowners entering retirement with mortgage debt often face increased financial pressure because fixed retirement income must still support housing obligations. Eliminating the mortgage before retirement can dramatically improve financial security and reduce stress later in life. This is one reason why many homeowners aggressively shorten loan terms during their peak earning years.

Some borrowers strategically refinance into shorter terms while maintaining investments simultaneously. Others prioritize total debt elimination before increasing investment contributions substantially. Both approaches can work depending on individual risk tolerance, investment philosophy, and financial goals. The important point is intentionality. Mortgage decisions should align with broader financial planning rather than operating independently.

Interest rate environments also influence loan term decisions. During periods of low rates, some borrowers prefer maintaining longer loans while investing excess cash elsewhere. Others still prioritize shorter terms because they value guaranteed debt elimination more than potential market returns. Neither approach is universally correct. The key is understanding the trade-offs involved.

One powerful strategy involves refinancing into a shorter-term loan while avoiding lifestyle inflation. Lifestyle inflation occurs when increasing income automatically leads to increasing expenses. Many homeowners receive raises or bonuses over time but expand spending proportionally, preventing meaningful financial progress. Instead, borrowers can redirect increased income toward accelerated mortgage repayment without significantly reducing quality of life because they were previously living on lower income levels already.

Psychology plays a major role in loan term success. Shorter loan terms often create stronger financial focus because the payoff timeline feels tangible and achievable. Borrowers become more intentional with spending decisions because they can clearly see the connection between discipline today and freedom tomorrow. Momentum builds as balances decline visibly faster.

Longer loan terms, while comfortable monthly, sometimes encourage complacency. Because payoff feels distant, borrowers may become less motivated to accelerate progress.

Years pass quickly, and many homeowners eventually realize they are still deeply in debt much later in life than expected. This is why active mortgage management matters so much.

Choosing the right loan term also impacts risk exposure. The longer debt exists, the longer borrowers remain vulnerable to economic disruptions, job losses, health emergencies, and financial uncertainty. Eliminating debt sooner reduces these risks substantially. Mortgage freedom increases resilience because households require less income to maintain stability.

At the same time, borrowers must avoid becoming "house poor" by selecting loan terms that create excessive strain. Aggressive payoff strategies should strengthen financial stability, not weaken it. Emergency savings, retirement contributions, insurance protection, and overall cash flow health must remain priorities. Sustainable progress is always more powerful than temporary intensity followed by financial burnout.

Throughout history, financially successful individuals often treated debt repayment strategically rather than emotionally. They understood that time magnifies financial decisions dramatically. A slightly more aggressive loan structure today may produce enormous freedom years later. Choosing the right loan term is not simply about monthly payments. It is about designing your financial future intentionally.

Every refinance creates a choice. Homeowners can either continue stretching debt across decades or reposition themselves toward faster ownership and reduced interest costs. The decision affects not only finances but also lifestyle flexibility, retirement readiness, stress levels, investment opportunities, and long-term wealth creation. Ultimately, the right loan term is the one that balances progress with sustainability. It should challenge the borrower enough to accelerate meaningful financial growth while remaining realistic enough to maintain consistency over time. Mortgage freedom is rarely achieved through luck. It is achieved through intentional decisions repeated consistently year after year.

When homeowners truly understand how loan terms shape financial outcomes, they begin viewing mortgages differently. The mortgage is no longer just a payment. It becomes a system that can either delay or accelerate freedom depending on how it is structured. Choosing the right loan term is one of the most important steps toward taking control of that system and reclaiming ownership of your financial future.

The Fifteen-Year Decision

Derrick and Amanda believed they were financially successful. They owned a beautiful home in a growing suburban neighborhood, drove newer vehicles, contributed to retirement accounts, and earned solid incomes. Derrick worked as an engineering consultant while Amanda owned a small interior design business. By most standards, they were doing well.

Yet beneath the surface, something bothered Derrick constantly. Every month, despite their income, the mortgage payment felt like a permanent shadow hanging over their lives. They had purchased the home with a thirty-year mortgage nearly seven years earlier. At the time, the payment felt reasonable and manageable. But as the years passed, Derrick became increasingly frustrated by how slowly the balance declined.

One evening, while reviewing their annual financial statements, he noticed something alarming.

They had already paid well over six figures toward the mortgage since purchasing the house, yet the balance remained shockingly high.

“That doesn’t even make sense,” Derrick muttered.

Amanda leaned over his shoulder.

“How much have we actually paid toward principal?”

Derrick clicked through the amortization schedule silently.

“Not nearly enough.”

For the first time, they truly understood how much interest dominated the early years of their mortgage.

Amanda sighed.

“It feels like we’re working for the bank.”

That sentence stayed with Derrick for days.

At work, he began researching mortgage structures obsessively during lunch breaks. He studied amortization schedules, refinance calculators, and long-term payoff strategies. What shocked him most was realizing how much power loan terms had over total repayment costs.

The thirty-year mortgage that once felt safe suddenly looked expensive and inefficient.

One night, Derrick showed Amanda two side-by-side comparisons on his laptop.

The first showed their current mortgage path. If they continued making minimum payments, they would remain in debt for another twenty-three years and pay an enormous amount in remaining interest.

The second scenario involved refinancing into a fifteen-year loan at a lower interest rate.

Amanda stared at the numbers carefully.

“That payment is higher,” she said cautiously.

“Yes,” Derrick admitted. “But look at the total interest difference.”

She leaned closer. The savings were staggering.

Not only would they eliminate the mortgage far sooner, but they would also save enough money in interest to completely change their long-term financial future.

Still, fear remained.

The higher payment felt intimidating. They worried about losing flexibility. Amanda’s business income fluctuated seasonally, and Derrick feared overcommitting financially.

For weeks, they debated the decision constantly.

Some friends encouraged them to keep the thirty-year mortgage and invest the difference instead. Others argued they should prioritize comfort and lower monthly obligations. Derrick understood both perspectives, but emotionally he could not shake the idea of remaining trapped in mortgage debt for decades longer.

One weekend, they sat together on the patio after dinner discussing the situation again.

Amanda finally asked a simple question.

"What do we actually want our life to look like fifteen years from now?"

The question shifted everything. They realized their true goal was not merely having lower payments today. They wanted freedom. They wanted options. They wanted the ability to travel, invest, reduce work stress, and eventually choose work because they enjoyed it rather than because massive obligations demanded it.

The next Monday, they moved forward with the refinance.

The process felt intimidating initially. They gathered documentation, reviewed disclosures, compared lenders, and analyzed every detail carefully. But when the refinance closed and the new fifteen-year mortgage officially replaced the old thirty-year loan, something changed psychologically.

For the first time, they had a clear finish line.

The early months required adjustment. The higher payment forced greater intentionality with spending. Dining out decreased. Impulse purchases disappeared almost entirely. Vacations became more strategic rather than extravagant.

Surprisingly, neither of them felt deprived.

Instead, they felt focused.

Every month, they watched the mortgage balance decline much faster than before. The difference was dramatic. Instead of barely reducing principal, large portions of every payment now attacked the balance directly. Derrick became fascinated by the progress.

"We're reducing more principal in one year than we used to reduce in three," he told Amanda excitedly one evening.

The momentum became addictive.

As Amanda's business grew, they resisted lifestyle inflation aggressively. Rather than upgrading cars or expanding spending habits, they applied additional income toward the mortgage. Bonuses, tax refunds, and side income all accelerated the payoff timeline further.

Their friends often questioned their discipline.

"You guys are too intense."

"Why not enjoy the money now?"

But Derrick and Amanda understood something deeper. Every extra payment was not just reducing debt. It was purchasing future freedom.

Then life tested them.

Three years into the fifteen-year mortgage, Derrick's company went through a major restructuring. Several coworkers lost their jobs unexpectedly. For the first time, Derrick experienced genuine fear about financial uncertainty.

But something surprised him.

Because they had aggressively reduced the mortgage balance already, maintained emergency savings, and controlled lifestyle inflation, they were far less vulnerable than many people around them.

Even if his income temporarily declined, they could survive.

That realization gave Derrick enormous peace of mind.

The refinance strategy had not merely accelerated debt payoff. It had strengthened their overall financial resilience.

Years passed faster than either of them expected.

The mortgage balance shrank aggressively year after year. Eventually, the remaining amount became so manageable that Amanda proposed something bold.

“What if we just finish it completely?”

They reviewed their investment balances, savings accounts, and cash reserves carefully. Because they had spent years building financial discipline, they now had options.

Six months later, they made the final mortgage payment.

The moment felt surreal.

Amanda sat quietly at the kitchen table staring at the confirmation screen online.

“It’s ours,” she whispered.

No lender. No mortgage statement. No decades of remaining debt.

The emotional impact overwhelmed them both.

That evening, they walked through every room in the house differently. For the first time, the home no longer represented obligation. It represented freedom.

The next few years transformed their lives completely.

Without a mortgage payment, cash flow expanded dramatically. Amanda grew her business without stress. Derrick reduced consulting hours and focused more on projects he genuinely enjoyed. They traveled extensively, increased investments aggressively, and helped support family members when needed.

Most importantly, they gained control over their time.

Looking back, Derrick realized the refinance itself was not the most important decision. The real turning point had been choosing a shorter loan term intentionally rather than accepting decades of debt automatically.

That one decision changed everything that followed.

Chapter 4

Refinancing Without Restarting the Mortgage Clock

One of the greatest misconceptions surrounding mortgage refinancing is the belief that refinancing always means "starting over." Many homeowners fear that refinancing will erase years of progress and trap them into another thirty-year mortgage cycle. This concern prevents countless borrowers from taking advantage of lower interest rates, improved loan structures, and opportunities to accelerate financial freedom. While it is true that refinancing can restart the amortization process if handled incorrectly, refinancing does not automatically extend debt unnecessarily. In fact, when structured strategically, refinancing can significantly shorten the mortgage payoff timeline while reducing total interest costs at the same time.

To understand why many homeowners fear refinancing, it is important to understand how traditional mortgages operate. Most mortgages are amortized over long periods, commonly thirty years. During the early years of the loan, the majority of each payment goes toward interest rather than principal reduction. This means homeowners build equity slowly at first even while making large monthly payments consistently. Over time, more of the payment gradually shifts toward principal as the balance declines.

The problem occurs when homeowners repeatedly refinance into new long-term loans without considering how amortization resets. Each refinance begins a new loan schedule where interest once again dominates the early payments. As a result, some borrowers unknowingly spend decades paying mostly interest while making limited progress reducing principal. They feel relief from lower monthly payments temporarily but remain trapped in long-term debt far longer than expected.

This does not mean refinancing is harmful. The issue is not refinancing itself. The issue is refinancing without strategy. A refinance should always support a long-term objective rather than merely solving a short-term payment concern. Homeowners who understand how to refinance properly can lower interest rates, improve cash flow, accelerate equity growth, and shorten repayment timelines simultaneously.

The first step toward refinancing intelligently is understanding the remaining timeline on the existing mortgage. For example, imagine a homeowner who has already made eight years of payments on a thirty-year loan. Technically, that borrower has approximately twenty-two years remaining. If the homeowner refinances into another new thirty-year mortgage and only makes minimum payments, the repayment timeline becomes extended again. Instead of owing the home free and clear in twenty-two years, the borrower may now remain in debt for thirty additional years.

This extension dramatically increases total interest costs over time. Many borrowers overlook this because they focus only on the monthly payment reduction. However, monthly savings can become very expensive if they significantly lengthen the debt obligation.

The good news is that refinancing does not require restarting the mortgage clock negatively. One of the most effective strategies involves refinancing into a shorter loan term that matches or improves the remaining payoff schedule. For example, if a homeowner has twenty-two years remaining, they may refinance into a twenty-year or fifteen-year mortgage rather than beginning another thirty-year cycle.

This approach preserves progress already made while still capturing benefits such as lower interest rates or improved loan structures. In many cases, borrowers are surprised to discover that shorter-term refinances create manageable payments because lower rates offset much of the increase caused by shorter amortization periods.

A lower interest rate changes the entire financial structure of the loan. Less interest accrues monthly, meaning more of each payment reduces principal immediately. When this lower rate is combined with a shorter loan term, the payoff acceleration becomes powerful. Borrowers build equity faster while dramatically reducing total interest paid over time.

Another highly effective strategy involves refinancing into a new thirty-year loan for flexibility while voluntarily maintaining the original payoff schedule. This strategy works particularly well for borrowers who want lower required payments but still intend to eliminate debt aggressively.

For example, suppose a homeowner refinances and lowers the required payment from $3,200 monthly to $2,500 monthly. Instead of spending the extra $700 elsewhere, the borrower continues making payments near the original amount. The extra funds apply directly toward principal reduction. This preserves flexibility because the borrower can temporarily reduce payments during emergencies while still aggressively attacking the mortgage during stable financial periods.

Flexibility is an important advantage often overlooked in aggressive mortgage planning. Some homeowners become so focused on eliminating debt quickly that they overcommit financially and create unnecessary stress. Sustainable strategies are usually more effective than extreme approaches that become difficult to maintain long term. Refinancing strategically also allows homeowners to remove costly mortgage insurance. Borrowers who originally purchased homes with low down payments may have been required to pay private mortgage insurance or FHA mortgage insurance premiums. As equity increases through appreciation and principal reduction, refinancing into a conventional structure may eliminate these costs completely.

Removing mortgage insurance can free up hundreds of dollars monthly without increasing housing expenses. Many homeowners then redirect these savings toward additional principal reduction, accelerating payoff even faster.

Home equity plays a central role in refinance opportunities. Equity represents the portion of the property truly owned by the homeowner. As balances decline and property values rise, equity increases. Higher equity often improves refinance eligibility while lowering lender risk. Borrowers with strong equity positions frequently qualify for better rates and terms.

Some homeowners fear that refinancing somehow eliminates the equity or progress they have already built. This is not true unless additional debt is intentionally added through cash-out refinancing. The principal already paid remains paid.

Refinancing simply restructures the remaining balance under new terms. For example, if a borrower originally financed $500,000 and has reduced the balance to $380,000, refinancing does not reset the balance back to the original amount unless additional cash is borrowed intentionally. The refinance simply replaces the remaining balance with a new loan structure.

Cash-out refinancing deserves careful consideration because it can either strengthen or weaken financial positions depending on how the funds are used. Borrowing against equity to fund depreciating assets, luxury purchases, or lifestyle inflation often creates long-term financial damage. However, using equity strategically for investments, business opportunities, renovations that increase value, or consolidating high-interest debt may improve financial outcomes significantly.

Intentionality matters tremendously. Financially successful homeowners generally view refinancing as a strategic tool rather than emotional relief. Every refinance decision should align with broader goals such as financial freedom, wealth building, retirement planning, or cash flow optimization.

Another important concept is understanding break-even analysis. Refinancing involves closing costs including lender fees, appraisal expenses, title charges, escrow funding, and prepaid items. Borrowers should calculate how long it will take for monthly savings to exceed these upfront costs. For example, if refinancing costs $5,000 and saves $400 monthly, the break-even point occurs after approximately thirteen months. After that point, the borrower begins generating true financial savings. If the refinance also accelerates payoff or dramatically reduces long-term interest costs, the benefits may become even greater over time.

Technology now allows homeowners to analyze refinance scenarios with precision. Mortgage calculators can compare loan structures, project payoff timelines, evaluate interest savings, and model principal reduction strategies. Financial literacy tools empower borrowers to make far more informed decisions than previous generations.

Psychology also influences refinance success significantly. Homeowners who actively manage their mortgage often feel more financially empowered and motivated overall. Instead of viewing the mortgage as a permanent burden, they begin seeing it as a system that can be optimized intentionally. This shift in mindset often improves other financial behaviors such as budgeting, saving, investing, and reducing unnecessary spending.

Some homeowners avoid refinancing because they assume they waited too long or missed the opportunity. However, meaningful improvements may still exist even later in the mortgage timeline. Reducing interest costs, eliminating insurance premiums, shortening loan terms, or restructuring debt more efficiently can create valuable long-term benefits at many stages of homeownership.

Retirement planning connects closely with mortgage management as well. Carrying mortgage debt deep into retirement can create unnecessary financial stress and reduce flexibility. Refinancing strategically during peak earning years may help homeowners eliminate debt before retirement, strengthening long-term security substantially.

At the same time, refinancing decisions should always remain balanced. Aggressively pursuing mortgage freedom should not come at the expense of emergency savings, retirement contributions, or overall financial stability. A healthy strategy balances debt reduction with liquidity and resilience.

One of the most powerful realizations homeowners can experience is understanding that the mortgage timeline is not fixed permanently. The original loan structure is simply a starting point. Through refinancing, principal reduction, payment optimization, and strategic planning, borrowers can reshape the timeline dramatically.

The mortgage clock belongs to the homeowner, not the bank. When homeowners stop treating refinancing as a temporary payment adjustment and begin treating it as a long-term financial strategy, everything changes. They stop focusing solely on monthly obligations and begin focusing on total wealth creation, financial flexibility, and freedom.

Ultimately, refinancing without restarting the mortgage clock requires awareness, discipline, and intentional planning. It requires understanding amortization, interest dynamics, loan terms, and long-term financial objectives. Most importantly, it requires rejecting the passive belief that mortgage debt must automatically last thirty years.

Mortgage freedom is not determined by the original loan documents. It is determined by the borrower's strategy and consistency over time.

When refinancing is used intelligently, it becomes one of the most powerful tools available for accelerating financial independence, reducing unnecessary interest, and reclaiming control over the future.

Refinancing Without Extending the Timeline

Let's look at a realistic example of how refinancing can lower interest costs without restarting the mortgage clock negatively.

Original Mortgage

A homeowner purchases a property with the following loan:

- Loan Amount: $450,000
- Interest Rate: 7.25%
- Loan Term: 30 Years
- Monthly Principal & Interest Payment: Approximately $3,069

After making payments for 8 years, the borrower still owes approximately:

- Remaining Balance: $403,000
- Remaining Loan Term: 22 Years

At this point, mortgage rates decline significantly.

The homeowner has two refinance options:

Option 1: Refinance Into a New 30-Year Mortgage

- New Loan Balance: $403,000
- New Interest Rate: 5.25%
- New Loan Term: 30 Years
- New Monthly Payment: Approximately $2,225

At first glance, this looks attractive because the payment drops by:

$3,069 - $2,225 = $844 monthly savings

However, there is a major issue.

The borrower now extends the loan from 22 remaining years back to 30 years.

Total Future Interest Paid

Approximate future interest on this new refinance:

- Total Payments Over 30 Years:

$2{,}225 \times 360 = 801{,}000$

- Minus Loan Balance:

$801{,}000 - 403{,}000 = 398{,}000$

Approximate future interest paid:

$398,000

Option 2: Refinance Into a 20-Year Mortgage

Instead, the borrower refinances strategically:

- New Loan Balance: $403,000
- New Interest Rate: 5.00%
- New Loan Term: 20 Years
- New Monthly Payment: Approximately $2,660

Now compare the numbers.

The payment only increases about:

$$2{,}660 - 2{,}225 = 435$$

Compared to Option 1.

But look at the long-term savings.

Total Future Interest Paid

- Total Payments Over 20 Years:

$$2{,}660 \times 240 = 638{,}400$$

- Minus Loan Balance:

638,400−403,000=235,400

Approximate future interest paid:

$235,400

Interest Savings Comparison

Option 1 Future Interest:

$398,000

Option 2 Future Interest:

$235,400

Total Interest Saved

398,000−235,400=162,600

By choosing the shorter refinance term strategically, the borrower saves approximately:

$162,600 in future interest

while paying off the home 10 years earlier.

Optional Accelerated Strategy

Suppose the homeowner chooses Option 1 for flexibility but continues making the old payment of $3,069 monthly instead of the new required payment of $2,225.

Extra principal paid monthly:

3,069−2,225=844

That extra $844 attacks principal directly every month.

Using this strategy, the borrower could potentially pay off the loan in roughly 18–20 years instead of 30 while still having the safety of the lower required payment during emergencies.

This demonstrates one of the most important lessons in mortgage refinancing:

The loan term printed on paper does not determine the actual payoff timeline.

Your strategy does.

Chapter 5

Using Refinancing to Eliminate High-Interest Debt Faster

For many homeowners, the mortgage is not the only debt affecting their financial future. Credit cards, personal loans, auto loans, student loans, business debt, and other financial obligations often consume a significant portion of monthly income. In many cases, these debts carry much higher interest rates than mortgage financing. While a mortgage may have an interest rate between five and eight percent depending on the market, credit cards frequently charge twenty percent or more annually. Personal loans and unsecured debt can also carry extremely expensive rates that quietly drain wealth month after month.

One of the most powerful but misunderstood uses of refinancing is the ability to strategically consolidate high-interest debt into a lower-cost mortgage structure. When approached intelligently, refinancing can dramatically improve cash flow, reduce total interest expenses, simplify financial management, and accelerate long-term debt elimination. However, when used irresponsibly, debt consolidation through refinancing can also create major financial problems. The difference depends entirely on discipline, intentionality, and long-term strategy.

Understanding the true cost of high-interest debt is essential. Many borrowers focus only on minimum monthly payments without realizing how much interest accumulates over time. Credit card companies are especially effective at creating the illusion of affordability by requiring relatively small minimum payments while allowing balances to linger for years or even decades. Meanwhile, large portions of every payment disappear toward interest charges rather than reducing the actual balance significantly.

For example, a borrower carrying multiple credit card balances at twenty-two percent interest may spend years making payments while seeing little meaningful progress. High-interest debt creates a financial drag that slows wealth creation dramatically. Every dollar flowing toward unnecessary interest becomes money unavailable for savings, investing, business opportunities, retirement planning, or principal reduction on appreciating assets.

Mortgage debt operates differently because it is secured by real estate and generally carries lower interest rates. This lower cost of borrowing creates an opportunity. By refinancing strategically and consolidating expensive debt into a lower-rate mortgage structure, borrowers may dramatically reduce interest expenses while simplifying repayment.

However, this strategy must be approached with caution and discipline. Refinancing to pay off high-interest debt is not about creating permission to spend more. It is about restructuring existing debt more efficiently. If borrowers consolidate debt but continue accumulating new balances afterward, the situation often becomes worse than before. The mortgage balance increases while new consumer debt reappears, creating double financial pressure.

This is why behavior matters more than mathematics alone. Refinancing can improve the structure of debt, but it cannot fix destructive spending habits automatically. True financial progress requires both strategic restructuring and disciplined money management moving forward.

One of the primary advantages of consolidating high-interest debt into a refinance is cash flow improvement. High-interest debts often require large monthly payments spread across multiple lenders. Consolidating these obligations into a lower-rate mortgage may reduce total monthly obligations substantially. This improved cash flow can create breathing room that allows homeowners to rebuild savings, invest consistently, or accelerate debt repayment further.

For example, a homeowner carrying $60,000 in credit card and personal loan debt at interest rates between eighteen and twenty-four percent may struggle to make meaningful progress despite large monthly payments. Refinancing the mortgage to consolidate that debt into a lower-rate structure may reduce interest costs dramatically while creating a more manageable repayment system.

Still, homeowners must understand the trade-offs involved. Unsecured debt such as credit cards becomes secured against the property once consolidated into the mortgage. This means the home itself becomes tied to the debt. Missing mortgage payments carries far greater consequences than missing unsecured credit card payments because foreclosure becomes a potential risk. This is why refinancing for debt consolidation should only be pursued when borrowers are committed to changing financial habits permanently.

One effective strategy involves refinancing while simultaneously implementing aggressive debt elimination systems. Instead of simply enjoying lower payments, disciplined borrowers redirect monthly savings toward principal reduction, emergency savings, or investments. This prevents the refinance from becoming merely temporary relief.

Another powerful benefit of refinancing high-interest debt involves improving psychological clarity. Many borrowers feel overwhelmed managing numerous payments across multiple accounts with varying due dates, interest rates, and minimum requirements. Consolidation simplifies the financial structure into a single organized system. This simplicity often reduces stress and improves consistency.

Stress reduction itself can create significant benefits. Financial anxiety affects decision-making, relationships, productivity, health, and emotional well-being. Homeowners carrying large amounts of high-interest debt often feel trapped despite earning solid incomes because interest consumes so much of their cash flow. Refinancing strategically can create emotional relief that improves overall financial focus and confidence.

Interest rate differentials are what make debt consolidation through refinancing potentially so powerful. Consider the difference between paying twenty-two percent interest on credit cards versus six percent mortgage interest. The gap is enormous. High-interest debt compounds aggressively against borrowers. Lower-interest mortgage structures slow this compounding dramatically, allowing more money to reduce principal rather than servicing interest. Still, homeowners should avoid viewing refinancing as a magical solution. Some borrowers repeatedly consolidate debt through refinancing without addressing the underlying causes of overspending. They pay off credit cards through refinancing only to rebuild balances again within a few years. This cycle can become extremely dangerous because mortgage balances increase while consumer debt returns simultaneously.

Financial discipline must accompany consolidation strategies. Borrowers should ideally reduce unnecessary spending, establish emergency reserves, improve budgeting systems, and eliminate destructive financial habits before or during the refinance process.

Emergency savings are especially important. Many people accumulate high-interest debt not because of irresponsible luxury spending but because they lack financial reserves during emergencies. Medical bills, job interruptions, vehicle repairs, or unexpected expenses force borrowers onto credit cards repeatedly. Without emergency savings, the cycle continues indefinitely.

Refinancing can provide an opportunity to reset financially, but only if accompanied by structural behavioral changes. Homeowners who build emergency reserves after consolidating debt often avoid returning to high-interest borrowing in the future. Another important consideration is loan term structure. Some borrowers consolidate debt into a new thirty-year mortgage and focus only on lowering payments. While this may improve short-term affordability, extending debt repayment excessively can increase long-term costs substantially. Strategic borrowers often combine debt consolidation with accelerated payoff strategies to avoid unnecessary interest accumulation over decades.

For example, a borrower may refinance into a twenty-year mortgage rather than restarting another full thirty-year cycle. Others may refinance into longer terms for flexibility while voluntarily continuing to make larger payments aggressively. The key is maintaining intentionality rather than allowing the refinance to become an excuse for financial complacency.

Home equity plays a central role in debt consolidation refinancing. Borrowers generally need sufficient equity to access cash through refinancing. Higher equity levels improve eligibility and may produce better loan terms. Rising property values often create opportunities for homeowners to restructure finances more efficiently.

Cash-out refinancing is one of the most common tools used for debt consolidation. In this structure, the borrower replaces the current mortgage with a larger loan and receives the difference in cash. Those funds are then used to pay off higher-interest obligations. The new mortgage balance becomes larger, but the overall debt structure may become far more manageable and cost-efficient.

Closing costs must also be evaluated carefully. Refinancing involves lender fees, appraisal charges, title expenses, escrow funding, and other transaction costs. Borrowers should calculate whether the interest savings and cash flow improvements justify these expenses over time.

Break-even analysis remains essential. If refinancing costs $8,000 but saves $1,200 monthly across multiple debts, the break-even period may occur within only several months. Long-term savings could then become substantial. However, every scenario should be evaluated individually rather than emotionally.

Credit improvement often follows successful debt consolidation strategies as well. Paying off revolving credit card balances may improve credit utilization ratios significantly, which can positively impact credit scores over time. Improved credit may later create additional financial opportunities including better financing terms, lower insurance costs, and stronger borrowing power.

Retirement planning also benefits from reducing high-interest debt. Borrowers trapped under large consumer debt obligations often struggle to invest consistently for the future.

Lowering interest costs through refinancing may free up cash flow that can be redirected toward retirement accounts, investment portfolios, or business growth.

Some homeowners also use refinancing strategically to eliminate auto loans, business loans, or private student loans carrying particularly high rates. Again, intentionality matters. The refinance should ideally improve overall financial efficiency rather than simply delaying repayment indefinitely.

Financial freedom rarely comes from income alone. Many high earners remain financially stressed because inefficient debt structures consume enormous portions of their cash flow. Wealth is often built through optimization rather than raw income increases. Lowering interest costs is one of the most effective optimization strategies available.

One important psychological shift homeowners must make is understanding that not all debt is equal. Debt attached to appreciating assets at lower rates may function very differently from high-interest consumer debt financing depreciating purchases. Strategic refinancing helps reorganize debt into more efficient structures aligned with long-term financial goals.

Ultimately, refinancing to eliminate high-interest debt faster is about reclaiming control. It is about reducing financial drag, improving efficiency, simplifying obligations, and creating momentum toward stability and freedom. When combined with discipline and intentional financial behavior, this strategy can dramatically accelerate wealth building and reduce years of financial stress.

The refinance itself is not the solution. The refinance is the tool. The real transformation occurs when borrowers pair strategic restructuring with long-term behavioral change. That combination creates the possibility for genuine financial freedom.

Using Refinancing to Eliminate High-Interest Debt

Let's look at a realistic example of how refinancing can dramatically reduce interest costs and accelerate debt payoff.

Current Financial Situation

A homeowner currently has:

Existing Mortgage

- Mortgage Balance: $350,000
- Interest Rate: 7.00%
- Remaining Loan Term: 25 Years

- Monthly Principal & Interest Payment: Approximately $2,474

Additional High-Interest Debt

Credit Cards

- Balance: $40,000
- Interest Rate: 22%
- Minimum Payment: Approximately $1,000 monthly

Personal Loan

- Balance: $20,000
- Interest Rate: 15%
- Monthly Payment: $475

Auto Loan

- Balance: $25,000
- Interest Rate: 10%
- Monthly Payment: $530

Total Monthly Debt Payments

Mortgage:

$2,474

Credit Cards:

$1,000

Personal Loan:

$475

Auto Loan:

$530

Total Monthly Debt Payments

2,474+1,000+475+530=4,479

Total monthly obligations:

$4,479

Refinancing Strategy

The homeowner decides to complete a cash-out refinance to consolidate all high-interest debt into the mortgage.

New Refinance Structure

New Mortgage Balance

Original Mortgage:

$350,000

Credit Cards:

$40,000

Personal Loan:

$20,000

Auto Loan:

$25,000

Estimated Closing Costs:

$10,000

Total New Mortgage

350,000+40,000+20,000+25,000+10,000=445,000

New mortgage balance:

$445,000

New Loan Terms

- New Interest Rate: 5.75%
- Loan Term: 25 Years

New Monthly Principal & Interest Payment

Approximately:

$2,804 monthly

Monthly Cash Flow Improvement

Old Total Monthly Debt Payments:

$4,479

New Mortgage Payment:

$2,804

Monthly Savings

4,479−2,804=1,675

Monthly cash flow improvement:

$1,675

Strategic Financial Decision

Now the homeowner has two choices.

Choice 1: Spend the Savings

If the borrower spends the extra $1,675 monthly on lifestyle upgrades, the refinance may create only temporary relief while risking future debt accumulation.

OR

Choice 2: Use the Savings Strategically

The borrower instead applies:

- $800 monthly toward extra mortgage principal
- $500 monthly into retirement investments
- $375 monthly into emergency savings

This transforms the refinance into a wealth-building strategy rather than simply debt reshuffling.

Accelerated Mortgage Payoff Example

Suppose the homeowner applies an additional $800 monthly toward principal.

Extra Annual Principal Reduction:

800×12=9,600

Extra principal reduction yearly:

$9,600

Over time, this dramatically accelerates payoff while reducing future interest.

Instead of remaining trapped under high-interest debt with minimal progress, the borrower now:

- Simplifies finances
- Reduces interest costs dramatically
- Improves cash flow
- Builds savings
- Accelerates mortgage payoff
- Creates long-term financial stability

Interest Rate Comparison

Credit Card Interest Example

On $40,000 at 22% interest:

Approximate annual interest:

$40{,}000 \times 0.22 = 8{,}800$

Approximate yearly interest:

$8,800

Mortgage Interest Example

That same $40,000 consolidated into a 5.75% mortgage structure:

Approximate annual interest:

$40{,}000 \times 0.0575 = 2{,}300$

Approximate yearly interest:

$2,300

Approximate Interest Savings

$8{,}800 - 2{,}300 = 6{,}500$

Approximate annual interest savings on that portion alone:

$6,500 yearly

This example demonstrates why strategic refinancing can become such a powerful financial tool.

The key lesson is this:

Refinancing high-interest debt only creates long-term success if the borrower changes the financial behaviors that created the debt originally.

When combined with discipline, refinancing can completely transform a household's financial future.

Chapter 6

Cash-Out Refinancing for Wealth Building and Mortgage Acceleration

Cash-out refinancing is one of the most powerful financial tools available to homeowners, yet it is also one of the most misunderstood. Some people view cash-out refinancing as dangerous because they associate it with overspending, consumer debt, or financial irresponsibility. Others see it as a shortcut to wealth without fully understanding the risks involved. The truth is that cash-out refinancing is neither inherently good nor bad. Like any financial tool, its effectiveness depends entirely on how it is used.

When approached strategically, cash-out refinancing can accelerate wealth building, improve cash flow, create investment opportunities, eliminate higher-interest debt, fund business growth, acquire income-producing assets, and even shorten the overall path to financial freedom. However, when used carelessly, it can also increase debt burdens, extend repayment timelines, and weaken long-term financial stability. Understanding the difference is essential for homeowners who want to use home equity intelligently rather than emotionally. To understand cash-out refinancing properly, homeowners must first understand home equity itself. Equity represents the portion of a property that the homeowner truly owns. It is the difference between the property's current market value and the remaining mortgage balance. As mortgage balances decline and property values appreciate over time, equity grows. In many cases, homeowners build substantial equity without fully realizing how valuable it can become.

For example, imagine a homeowner purchased a property for $400,000 several years ago with a mortgage balance of $360,000. Over time, the property appreciates to $550,000 while the mortgage balance declines to $310,000. The homeowner now has approximately $240,000 in equity. This equity represents financial power that can potentially be leveraged strategically.

Cash-out refinancing allows homeowners to access part of this equity by replacing the existing mortgage with a larger new loan. The previous mortgage is paid off, and the borrower receives the difference in cash. This cash can then be used for a variety of financial purposes depending on the homeowner's goals and strategy.

The key issue is not whether equity should be accessed. The key issue is what the equity is being used for.

Using home equity to purchase depreciating assets, fund luxury consumption, or support unsustainable lifestyles often creates long-term financial damage. Borrowers who repeatedly extract equity to finance cars, vacations, entertainment, or excessive spending habits frequently weaken their financial future significantly. They increase debt while failing to create assets or income that improve long-term stability.

In contrast, homeowners who use cash-out refinancing strategically often treat equity as investment capital. They deploy funds into opportunities capable of generating income, appreciation, or long-term financial growth. This distinction changes everything.

One of the most common wealth-building uses for cash-out refinancing is acquiring income-producing real estate. Some homeowners refinance primary residences to access capital for down payments on rental properties, short-term rentals, duplexes, triplexes, or small multifamily investments. When these properties generate positive cash flow and appreciate over time, the refinance can potentially create wealth far beyond the cost of the borrowed funds.

For example, a homeowner may access $100,000 in equity through refinancing and use it as a down payment on an investment property producing monthly rental income. If the property appreciates while tenants help pay down the mortgage balance, the homeowner may build wealth much faster than by leaving the equity unused inside the primary residence.

Another strategic use involves funding business expansion. Entrepreneurs often struggle to access affordable business capital, especially during early growth phases. Credit cards, unsecured loans, and alternative financing frequently carry extremely high interest rates. In some situations, using lower-cost mortgage financing to fund a carefully planned business expansion may create significant long-term financial improvement.

Again, intentionality is critical. Borrowing against home equity for speculative or poorly planned business ventures introduces risk. However, using equity strategically to expand stable cash-flowing operations, acquire productive equipment, increase marketing capacity, or improve operational efficiency may strengthen financial outcomes substantially.

Cash-out refinancing can also support home improvements that increase property value or improve long-term livability. Renovations such as kitchen upgrades, bathroom remodels, additional living space, energy-efficient systems, or property improvements may increase both quality of life and long-term equity. However, homeowners should evaluate renovation costs carefully and avoid over-improving properties beyond neighborhood value ranges unnecessarily. One of the most important concepts homeowners must understand is leverage. Leverage refers to using borrowed money to potentially increase returns. Real estate investors and financially sophisticated individuals often use leverage strategically because it allows them to control larger assets with less initial cash. Mortgage financing itself is a form of leverage.

Cash-out refinancing increases leverage because the homeowner borrows against accumulated equity. This can magnify gains if the borrowed funds are used productively. However, it can also magnify losses if used irresponsibly. This is why risk management becomes essential.

Risk management begins with maintaining financial stability. Homeowners should avoid extracting excessive equity that creates unmanageable mortgage payments or leaves insufficient emergency reserves. Liquidity matters. Even strong investments can become problematic if borrowers lack adequate cash flow or reserves during economic disruptions.

Interest rates also play a central role in cash-out refinance decisions. Borrowing at lower mortgage rates may be far cheaper than alternative financing sources. For example, mortgage interest rates may remain substantially lower than credit card rates, business loans, or unsecured borrowing options. This lower cost of capital creates opportunities for strategic financial optimization.

Still, homeowners must evaluate the spread between borrowing costs and expected returns carefully. If borrowed funds are invested into opportunities producing stronger returns than the mortgage interest rate, wealth may grow more efficiently over time. However, expected returns are never guaranteed. Risk must always be considered honestly.

Some homeowners use cash-out refinancing strategically to eliminate high-interest consumer debt before redirecting future cash flow toward investments and accelerated mortgage reduction. This combination can improve financial efficiency dramatically if accompanied by disciplined financial habits moving forward.

Another powerful strategy involves using cash-out refinancing to create multiple streams of income. Many financially successful individuals focus heavily on building cash-flow-producing assets because income diversification increases long-term stability. Rental properties, businesses, dividend-producing investments, and other income sources may strengthen financial resilience substantially.

The psychological impact of building additional income streams can also be transformative. Homeowners who create investments generating monthly cash flow often feel less dependent on single employment sources. This increased flexibility may reduce stress and create greater control over life decisions.

However, homeowners must avoid becoming overleveraged. Overleveraging occurs when debt obligations become too large relative to income, reserves, or asset stability. Excessive leverage creates vulnerability during economic downturns, vacancies, market declines, or unexpected expenses. Sustainable leverage is far more powerful than reckless expansion.

One important advantage of real estate-backed borrowing is predictability. Fixed-rate mortgages create stable payment structures over long periods of time. This allows borrowers to plan strategically. In contrast, many alternative financing sources carry variable rates, shorter terms, or unstable payment structures.

Tax considerations may also influence cash-out refinance decisions depending on individual circumstances and evolving tax laws. Borrowers should always consult qualified tax professionals when evaluating large refinance strategies involving investments, businesses, or significant debt restructuring. Timing matters as well. Property appreciation cycles, interest rate environments, rental demand, and economic conditions all influence refinance opportunities. Some homeowners access equity during strong appreciation periods to expand investments strategically before rates rise further. Others prioritize paying down debt aggressively during uncertain markets. Flexibility and awareness remain essential.

Closing costs must also be evaluated carefully. Cash-out refinances involve lender fees, title expenses, appraisals, escrow adjustments, and other transaction costs. These costs should be weighed against the expected long-term financial benefits generated by the refinance strategy.

Break-even analysis remains important. If the refinance funds are used productively to create appreciation, income, or substantial interest savings, the long-term benefits may far exceed upfront transaction costs. However, every scenario should be analyzed realistically rather than emotionally.

Some homeowners fear using equity because they view debt emotionally rather than strategically. While caution is wise, fear alone should not prevent intelligent financial decisions. Wealthy individuals often use debt strategically because they understand how to deploy capital productively while managing risk carefully.

At the same time, homeowners should never assume rising property values alone guarantee safety. Real estate markets fluctuate. Cash-flow management and conservative planning remain essential regardless of market optimism.

One of the most powerful concepts in wealth building is opportunity cost. Opportunity cost refers to what is sacrificed by choosing one option over another. Leaving large amounts of equity idle inside a property may sometimes represent a missed opportunity if those funds could generate stronger returns elsewhere. However, maintaining strong equity positions also creates stability and security. The balance depends on the homeowner's goals, risk tolerance, and financial strategy.

Cash-out refinancing should never be approached impulsively. It requires careful planning, honest risk assessment, disciplined execution, and long-term vision. Homeowners should understand exactly how the funds will be used before refinancing occurs.

Most importantly, the refinance should ideally create assets, cash flow, or financial efficiency that improve long-term positioning rather than simply increasing consumption.

Ultimately, cash-out refinancing is not about borrowing more money merely because equity exists. It is about converting dormant equity into productive financial energy. When used intelligently, it can accelerate wealth creation, expand opportunities, strengthen cash flow, and shorten the path toward financial freedom.

The key is understanding that home equity is not simply a number on paper. It is a financial resource that can either remain passive or become part of a larger wealth-building strategy depending on how the homeowner chooses to use it.

Using Cash-Out Refinancing to Build Wealth

Let's look at a realistic example of how cash-out refinancing can be used strategically for wealth building and mortgage acceleration.

Current Property Situation

A homeowner purchased a primary residence several years ago.

Current Property Value

- Home Value: $700,000

Current Mortgage

- Remaining Mortgage Balance: $350,000

- Current Interest Rate: 6.75%
- Remaining Loan Term: 24 Years
- Current Monthly Principal & Interest Payment: Approximately $2,610

Because the property appreciated substantially over time, the homeowner now has:

Total Equity

700,000−350,000=350,000

Total equity:

$350,000

Cash-Out Refinance Strategy

The homeowner decides to complete a cash-out refinance to access investment capital.

New Refinance Structure

- New Loan Amount: $500,000
- Cash Received After Paying Off Existing Mortgage:

500,000−350,000=150,000

Cash available before closing costs:

$150,000

Estimated closing costs:

$10,000

Net Cash Available

150,000–10,000=140,000

Net cash received:

$140,000

Investment Strategy

The homeowner uses the $140,000 strategically:

Rental Property Down Payment

- Down Payment: $100,000

Emergency Investment Reserve

- Cash Reserves: $20,000

Renovations on Rental Property

- Improvements: $20,000

Rental Property Purchase

Rental Property Price

- Purchase Price: $400,000

Mortgage on Rental Property

- Loan Amount: $300,000
- Interest Rate: 6.50%
- Monthly Principal & Interest Payment: Approximately $1,896

Rental Income

Monthly rental income:

$3,200

Estimated monthly expenses:

- Taxes/Insurance: $600
- Maintenance Reserve: $300
- Mortgage Payment: $1,896

Total Monthly Expenses

600+300+1,896=2,796

Total monthly expenses:

$2,796

Monthly Cash Flow

Rental income:

$3,200

Minus expenses:

$2,796

Positive Monthly Cash Flow

3,200−2,796=404

Positive monthly cash flow:

$404 monthly

Annual Cash Flow

404×12=4,848

Annual positive cash flow:

$4,848

Long-Term Wealth Growth

Now let's add appreciation and principal reduction.

Suppose the rental property appreciates at an average of 4% annually.

First-Year Appreciation

$400{,}000 \times 0.04 = 16{,}000$

Approximate appreciation:

$16,000

Total First-Year Wealth Increase

Cash flow:

$4,848

Appreciation:

$16,000

Mortgage principal reduction (approximate):

$4,500

Total First-Year Wealth Increase

4,848+16,000+4,500=25,348

Approximate first-year wealth growth:

$25,348

Mortgage Impact on Primary Residence

The refinance increased the homeowner's primary mortgage balance from:

$350,000

to

$500,000

However, the borrowed equity is now generating:

- Positive cash flow
- Additional appreciation
- Additional principal reduction
- A second appreciating asset
- Increased long-term wealth potential

Strategic Accelerated Payoff Option

Suppose the homeowner applies the rental property cash flow toward the primary mortgage.

Additional annual mortgage reduction:

$4,848 yearly

Over time, this extra principal reduction can accelerate payoff significantly while the rental property itself continues appreciating and building equity.

Key Lesson

This example demonstrates the difference between:

Productive Debt

Borrowing against equity to acquire income-producing assets.

VERSUS

Destructive Debt

Borrowing against equity to fund depreciating purchases or lifestyle inflation.

The same refinance can either:

- Create long-term wealth and financial freedom

OR

- Create greater long-term financial stress

depending entirely on how the funds are used.

Cash-out refinancing becomes powerful when the borrowed money begins working for the homeowner instead of simply increasing consumption.

Chapter 7

Refinancing to Eliminate Mortgage Insurance and Increase Cash Flow

Mortgage insurance is one of the most overlooked expenses in homeownership. Many borrowers focus heavily on interest rates, monthly payments, and down payment requirements while paying little attention to the long-term cost of mortgage insurance premiums. Yet for millions of homeowners, mortgage insurance quietly drains hundreds of dollars every month without reducing the loan balance or building wealth. Over time, these costs can total tens of thousands of dollars that provide no direct financial return to the borrower.

Refinancing strategically can eliminate mortgage insurance entirely, creating immediate cash flow improvement while accelerating mortgage payoff and long-term wealth building. Understanding how mortgage insurance works, why lenders require it, and how refinancing can remove it is essential for homeowners who want to optimize their mortgage structure intelligently.

Mortgage insurance exists primarily to protect lenders, not borrowers. When borrowers purchase homes with smaller down payments, lenders assume greater risk because there is less homeowner equity protecting the property. To offset this risk, lenders require additional insurance premiums that compensate them if the borrower defaults on the loan.

There are several common forms of mortgage insurance. Conventional loans often require private mortgage insurance, commonly called PMI, when borrowers put less than twenty percent down. FHA loans require both upfront and ongoing mortgage insurance premiums, often referred to as MIP. USDA loans include guarantee fees, and some other specialized loan products carry similar risk-based insurance structures.

Many homeowners accept mortgage insurance as simply part of the homebuying process. In many cases, this is reasonable because lower down payment programs allow buyers to purchase homes sooner rather than waiting years to accumulate large down payments. Mortgage insurance can therefore provide access to homeownership earlier in life, which may still create long-term wealth benefits through appreciation and equity growth.

However, while mortgage insurance may help borrowers enter the housing market, it should not necessarily remain permanent. As equity grows over time, continuing to pay mortgage insurance often becomes financially inefficient.

Refinancing can provide an opportunity to eliminate these unnecessary costs and redirect the savings toward more productive financial goals.

The impact of mortgage insurance is often larger than homeowners initially realize. Some borrowers pay several hundred dollars monthly in PMI or FHA mortgage insurance premiums. Over five or ten years, the cumulative cost can become substantial. Unlike principal payments, mortgage insurance does not reduce the mortgage balance. Unlike property improvements, it does not increase home value. It is purely an expense designed to protect the lender's interests.

For example, a homeowner paying $350 monthly in mortgage insurance spends:

$350\times12=4{,}200$

$4,200 yearly

Over ten years, assuming no changes:

$4{,}200\times10=42{,}000$

$42,000 total

That money creates no ownership increase, no appreciation, and no wealth accumulation directly. This is why eliminating mortgage insurance strategically can become such a powerful financial improvement. Homeowners generally become eligible to remove mortgage insurance when sufficient equity exists in the property. Equity grows through two primary mechanisms: principal reduction and property appreciation. As mortgage balances decline and property values rise, the loan-to-value ratio improves. Lower loan-to-value ratios reduce lender risk substantially.

On conventional loans, PMI may sometimes be removed automatically once the loan reaches certain equity thresholds. However, many borrowers refinance before reaching automatic removal timelines because refinancing may also produce lower interest rates, improved loan terms, or additional strategic benefits simultaneously.

FHA mortgage insurance often operates differently. Many FHA borrowers continue paying mortgage insurance for the life of the loan unless they refinance into a conventional mortgage structure. This creates a major opportunity for homeowners whose property values have appreciated or whose loan balances have declined sufficiently over time.

For example, a borrower who originally purchased a home with minimal down payment using FHA financing may later refinance into a conventional loan after appreciation increases equity beyond twenty percent. Eliminating FHA mortgage insurance can produce dramatic monthly savings immediately.

Cash flow improvement is one of the most immediate benefits of removing mortgage insurance. Lower monthly obligations create financial breathing room that homeowners can use strategically. Some borrowers redirect savings toward accelerated mortgage principal payments. Others build emergency reserves, invest for retirement, purchase additional assets, or improve overall financial stability.

The key is intentionality. Simply spending the extra cash flow on lifestyle inflation may reduce the long-term impact of the refinance. However, redirecting the savings productively can create compounding financial improvement over time.

One powerful strategy involves applying the mortgage insurance savings directly toward principal reduction. Because the homeowner was already accustomed to making the higher payment previously, maintaining the same total payment feels psychologically manageable. Yet now, instead of paying insurance premiums, the extra funds reduce principal directly.

This accelerates equity growth substantially.

For example, suppose a homeowner eliminates $300 monthly in mortgage insurance through refinancing but continues paying the same total monthly amount voluntarily. That extra $300 now attacks principal instead of disappearing into insurance expenses. Annual additional principal reduction becomes:

$300 \times 12 = 3{,}600$

$3,600 yearly

Over time, this accelerated principal reduction compounds significantly because lower balances reduce future interest charges as well.

Interest rates also influence mortgage insurance refinance decisions. Sometimes borrowers refinance primarily to remove insurance while simultaneously lowering the interest rate. This combination creates a double financial benefit: reduced interest costs and eliminated insurance expenses. Together, these improvements may dramatically strengthen long-term mortgage efficiency.

However, homeowners should evaluate refinance costs carefully. Refinancing involves lender fees, appraisal expenses, title charges, escrow adjustments, and other transaction costs. The financial benefits of removing mortgage insurance should outweigh these costs over time.

Break-even analysis remains essential. Suppose refinancing

costs $6,000 but removes $400 monthly in mortgage insurance and interest savings combined. The break-even period would be approximately fifteen months. After that point, the homeowner begins generating true net savings.

Property appreciation plays a major role in refinance eligibility. In strong real estate markets, homeowners may build equity faster than expected simply because home values increase substantially over time. Some borrowers who initially believed they would carry mortgage insurance for many years discover refinance opportunities much sooner due to appreciation alone.

Still, homeowners should avoid depending entirely on appreciation. Markets fluctuate, and long-term financial strategies should remain conservative and sustainable. Principal reduction remains one of the most reliable methods for improving equity positions over time.

Credit improvement may also strengthen refinance opportunities. Borrowers who improve credit scores after purchasing homes often qualify for better refinance rates later. Stronger credit combined with increased equity may eliminate mortgage insurance while reducing interest costs simultaneously.

Mortgage insurance elimination can also create psychological benefits. Many homeowners feel frustrated knowing part of their payment protects the lender rather than improving their own financial position. Removing this expense often increases motivation and financial confidence because more of the payment now contributes directly toward ownership and equity.

Some homeowners choose to refinance into shorter loan terms while eliminating mortgage insurance simultaneously. This can accelerate mortgage payoff dramatically. Although monthly payments may remain similar or even increase slightly, the long-term interest savings and accelerated ownership timeline often become substantial.

For example, a borrower refinancing from a thirty-year FHA loan into a twenty-year conventional mortgage may eliminate mortgage insurance while reducing total repayment years significantly. This creates long-term financial efficiency even if monthly payments do not decline dramatically.

Another important factor is retirement planning. Eliminating unnecessary mortgage insurance improves long-term cash flow and reduces wasteful expenses. Homeowners approaching retirement especially benefit from improving mortgage efficiency because fixed retirement incomes operate more effectively when unnecessary debt costs are minimized.

Refinancing strategically also allows homeowners to reevaluate broader financial goals. Mortgage optimization should connect to investment planning, savings targets, business opportunities, lifestyle objectives, and overall wealth-building strategies. Every dollar saved from eliminated insurance premiums can potentially become capital for future growth.

One major mistake homeowners make is assuming mortgage insurance is unavoidable forever. In reality, mortgage insurance is often temporary when managed strategically. Homeowners who actively monitor equity growth, interest rates, and refinance opportunities frequently eliminate these costs years earlier than expected.

Education becomes critical here. Many borrowers never realize refinancing could remove mortgage insurance because lenders or loan servicers do not always proactively explain these opportunities. Financial literacy empowers homeowners to take control of their mortgage structure rather than simply accepting existing terms indefinitely.

Homeowners should also understand the emotional difference between productive and unproductive payments. Principal reduction builds ownership. Investments build assets. Savings create security. Mortgage insurance, by contrast, often produces no direct wealth accumulation for the borrower once sufficient equity exists.

This is why removing mortgage insurance can become such an important milestone financially and psychologically. Ultimately, refinancing to eliminate mortgage insurance is about improving efficiency. It is about redirecting money away from unnecessary lender protection costs and toward ownership, freedom, and long-term financial growth.

Mortgage insurance may help borrowers achieve homeownership initially, but it should not remain permanently without evaluation. Homeowners who monitor their equity positions carefully and refinance strategically can often save substantial amounts over time while accelerating their path toward mortgage freedom.

Every dollar no longer wasted on mortgage insurance becomes a dollar available for principal reduction, investing, savings, or wealth building. Over years and decades, these differences become life-changing.

The goal is not merely reducing expenses temporarily. The goal is creating a mortgage structure that maximizes long-term financial progress and minimizes unnecessary financial drag.

When homeowners understand how to eliminate mortgage insurance strategically, they take another major step toward reclaiming control over their financial future.

Eliminating Mortgage Insurance Through Refinancing

Let's look at a realistic example of how refinancing can eliminate mortgage insurance and improve long-term financial efficiency.

Original Home Purchase

A homeowner purchased a property using an FHA loan.

Purchase Price

- Home Price: $450,000

Down Payment

- Down Payment: 3.5%
- Down Payment Amount: Approximately $15,750

Original Mortgage

- Original Loan Amount: Approximately $434,250
- Interest Rate: 7.00%
- Loan Term: 30 Years

FHA Mortgage Insurance Premium (MIP)

- Monthly FHA Mortgage Insurance: $310 monthly

Original Principal & Interest Payment

Approximately:

$2,889 monthly

Total Original Monthly Housing Payment (Before Taxes & Insurance)

Mortgage Payment:

$2,889

Mortgage Insurance:

$310

Total Monthly Cost

2,889+310=3,199

Total monthly housing payment:

$3,199

Five Years Later

After five years:

Remaining Mortgage Balance

Approximately:

$405,000

Property Appreciation

The home value increased significantly.

Current appraised value:

$575,000

Current Equity Position

Home value:

$575,000

Remaining mortgage balance:

$405,000

Total Equity

575,000−405,000=170,000

Total equity:

$170,000

Current Loan-to-Value Ratio

Loan balance:

$405,000

Home value:

$575,000

Loan-to-Value Calculation

$405{,}000/575{,}000 \times 100 \approx 70.4\%$

Loan-to-value ratio:

Approximately 70%

Because the borrower now has well over 20% equity, they qualify for a conventional refinance without mortgage insurance.

New Refinance Structure

New Loan Amount

- $405,000

New Interest Rate

- 5.50%

New Loan Term

- 25 Years

New Principal & Interest Payment

Approximately:

$2,487 monthly

New Mortgage Insurance

$0

Mortgage insurance completely eliminated.

Monthly Savings Comparison

Old Payment Structure

Mortgage Payment:

$2,889

Mortgage Insurance:

$310

Total:

$3,199

New Payment Structure

New mortgage payment:

$2,487

Mortgage insurance:

$0

New Total Payment

$2,487

Total Monthly Savings

3,199−2,487=712

Monthly savings:

$712

Annual Savings

712×12=8,544

Annual savings:

$8,544

Strategic Principal Reduction Option

Suppose the homeowner chooses not to spend the savings.

Instead, they continue making the old payment amount of $3,199 monthly.

New required payment:

$2,487

Extra principal payment:

$3{,}199 - 2{,}487 = 712$

Additional monthly principal reduction:

$712

Annual Additional Principal Reduction

$712 \times 12 = 8{,}544$

Additional yearly principal reduction:

$8,544

Long-Term Impact

By eliminating mortgage insurance and continuing to make the original payment amount:

- Mortgage payoff accelerates dramatically
- Interest costs decline significantly
- Equity grows faster
- Cash flow flexibility improves
- Financial stress decreases
- Long-term wealth potential increases

Mortgage Insurance Waste Example

Suppose the homeowner kept the FHA loan and paid mortgage insurance for another 20 years.

Annual mortgage insurance cost:

$3,720 yearly

Total Future Mortgage Insurance Cost

$3{,}720 \times 20 = 74{,}400$

Potential future mortgage insurance expense:

$74,400

That money would not reduce the loan balance or increase ownership at all.

Key Lesson

This example demonstrates why refinancing to eliminate mortgage insurance can become such a powerful financial strategy.

The homeowner:

- Reduced the interest rate
- Eliminated mortgage insurance completely
- Improved monthly cash flow
- Accelerated principal reduction
- Increased long-term financial efficiency

Most importantly, money that once protected the lender now works directly toward building the homeowner's wealth and financial freedom.

Chapter 8

Refinancing Into a Shorter Loan Term for Massive Interest Savings

One of the most powerful mortgage strategies available to homeowners is refinancing into a shorter loan term. While many borrowers focus almost entirely on lowering monthly payments, financially disciplined homeowners often prioritize something far more valuable: reducing total interest paid and accelerating financial freedom. Refinancing into a shorter-term mortgage can dramatically reduce the amount of interest paid over time, shorten the debt timeline by years or even decades, and increase long-term wealth potential significantly.

Most homeowners underestimate how much interest truly costs over the life of a mortgage. A traditional thirty-year loan spreads repayment across decades, allowing lenders to collect interest for an extremely long period of time. While the monthly payment may appear manageable, the total long-term cost of borrowing often becomes enormous. This is why many financially successful individuals aggressively shorten loan terms whenever possible. They understand that time magnifies interest dramatically. Interest is essentially the cost of borrowing money. The longer debt exists, the more interest accumulates. Even relatively small interest rates become expensive when applied over thirty years. Many borrowers focus only on monthly affordability while ignoring the total repayment cost. This mindset often keeps homeowners trapped in debt far longer than necessary.

Refinancing into a shorter loan term changes the mathematics of the mortgage completely. Instead of spreading repayment across thirty years, the borrower compresses repayment into fifteen, twenty, or even ten years. Because the balance declines much faster, interest has less time to accumulate. This dramatically reduces total interest expenses while accelerating equity growth.

For example, a homeowner refinancing from a thirty-year mortgage into a fifteen-year loan may save hundreds of thousands of dollars in future interest depending on the loan size and interest rate. The payment may increase, but the long-term financial benefits can be extraordinary.

Many borrowers initially resist shorter loan terms because they focus emotionally on the higher monthly payment. However, this perspective often ignores the enormous opportunity cost of paying interest for decades unnecessarily. Every extra year of mortgage debt represents additional income flowing to lenders instead of remaining under the homeowner's control. One of the most important mindset shifts homeowners must make is understanding the difference between payment affordability and financial efficiency. Lower payments may improve short-term comfort, but they often increase long-term costs substantially. Higher payments, when structured sustainably, may dramatically strengthen long-term wealth creation by reducing interest and accelerating ownership.

The key word is sustainably. Refinancing into a shorter loan term should strengthen financial stability rather than create excessive pressure. Homeowners should maintain emergency reserves, retirement contributions, and overall cash flow health. The goal is intentional acceleration, not financial burnout.

One major advantage of shorter-term loans is that lenders often offer lower interest rates compared to longer-term mortgages. Fifteen-year loans frequently carry significantly lower rates than thirty-year loans because lenders face less long-term risk. This creates a double benefit: borrowers not only shorten repayment timelines but also reduce the interest rate itself.

The combination can become extremely powerful.

For example, suppose a homeowner currently has a thirty-year mortgage at seven percent interest. Refinancing into a fifteen-year loan at five and a half percent changes both the repayment timeline and the borrowing cost simultaneously. More of every payment reduces principal immediately while less interest accumulates overall.

This accelerated principal reduction creates momentum quickly. On shorter-term loans, a much larger percentage of each payment attacks the balance directly from the beginning. Borrowers often feel psychologically motivated because they can see meaningful progress almost immediately compared to slower-moving thirty-year amortization schedules.

Equity growth also accelerates substantially. Equity represents ownership in the property. Faster principal reduction means homeowners own more of the property sooner. This strengthens financial flexibility and may create future opportunities for investments, refinancing, or debt elimination strategies.

Another major benefit involves retirement planning. Carrying mortgage debt into retirement can create significant stress because fixed retirement income must continue supporting large housing payments. Eliminating mortgage debt earlier improves financial security dramatically later in life. Many homeowners strategically refinance into shorter terms during peak earning years specifically to eliminate debt before retirement. Cash flow management remains critical, however. Some homeowners become overly aggressive with shorter loan terms and create unnecessary strain. Financial resilience matters more than extreme intensity. The ideal refinance structure balances accelerated payoff with sustainable cash flow.

This is why some borrowers choose twenty-year loans instead of fifteen-year structures. Twenty-year mortgages still reduce interest dramatically compared to thirty-year loans while keeping payments more manageable. Others refinance into fifteen-year loans but maintain strong emergency reserves for flexibility.

Another powerful strategy involves refinancing into shorter terms while continuing to avoid lifestyle inflation. Lifestyle inflation occurs when income increases automatically lead to increased spending. Many homeowners earn substantially more money years after purchasing their homes but gradually expand spending habits rather than accelerating financial progress.

Refinancing into a shorter-term mortgage allows homeowners to redirect increased income toward ownership and freedom instead of unnecessary consumption. Because they previously survived on lower income levels, many borrowers can aggressively accelerate mortgage payoff without reducing overall quality of life substantially. Psychology plays a major role in the success of shorter-term refinancing strategies. Long-term debt often creates mental pressure even when payments remain affordable. Many homeowners feel trapped by the idea of owing mortgage payments for decades. In contrast, shorter loan terms create visible progress and tangible finish lines that motivate discipline and intentionality.

Some borrowers worry that refinancing into shorter terms prevents investing elsewhere. This concern deserves thoughtful consideration. Mortgage acceleration and investing are not necessarily mutually exclusive. Some financially successful individuals aggressively invest while maintaining longer mortgage structures. Others prioritize eliminating debt before expanding investments significantly.

Neither strategy is universally correct. The best approach depends on risk tolerance, investment philosophy, cash flow stability, age, and personal goals. However, one guaranteed benefit of shorter-term refinancing is reduced interest expense. Investment returns remain uncertain, but mortgage interest savings are mathematically predictable.

Interest savings themselves create wealth. Every dollar not paid to lenders remains available for future investing, savings, or lifestyle flexibility. Over decades, these savings compound significantly. Homeowners should also understand the relationship between inflation and fixed-rate debt. Some financial advisors argue that maintaining low-rate long-term debt during inflationary environments can be beneficial because future dollars become less valuable over time. While this argument has merit, many homeowners still prioritize the emotional and financial security of eliminating debt sooner.

There is no universal formula that fits every household. The important factor is intentionality. Mortgage decisions should support broader life goals rather than operating on autopilot.

Closing costs remain important considerations when refinancing into shorter terms. Refinancing involves appraisal fees, title expenses, lender charges, escrow funding, and other transaction costs. Homeowners should calculate whether the interest savings justify these expenses over time.

Break-even analysis helps evaluate this. If refinancing costs $7,000 but saves $1,000 monthly in long-term interest-equivalent value and accelerated principal reduction, the refinance may create enormous long-term value despite upfront costs.

Another important concept is optional acceleration. Some borrowers refinance into shorter terms while continuing to make additional principal payments voluntarily. Others refinance into slightly longer terms for flexibility while paying aggressively whenever possible. The exact structure matters less than the long-term consistency and intentionality behind the strategy.

One overlooked benefit of shorter-term mortgages is increased financial confidence. Homeowners aggressively reducing debt often become more disciplined in other areas of life as well. They budget more carefully, save more consistently, invest more intentionally, and avoid unnecessary liabilities. Financial momentum creates psychological momentum.

Economic uncertainty also highlights the value of reduced debt timelines. Homeowners carrying smaller balances and shorter obligations often feel more secure during recessions, job disruptions, or market instability. Lower debt exposure reduces vulnerability significantly.

Some homeowners assume they are "too late" to refinance into shorter terms because they already spent years on their mortgage. This is rarely true. Even later-stage refinances can produce meaningful savings if rates improve or repayment timelines shorten substantially. Financial progress is always valuable regardless of timing.

Mortgage freedom changes more than finances alone. It changes stress levels, career flexibility, lifestyle options, and long-term security. Homeowners without mortgage obligations often gain the ability to take entrepreneurial risks, reduce work hours, travel more freely, or support family members more comfortably.

Ultimately, refinancing into a shorter loan term is not merely about paying off a house faster. It is about reclaiming years of financial freedom. It is about reducing unnecessary interest, accelerating ownership, strengthening cash flow long term, and creating a more stable financial future.

The mortgage term printed on paper influences decades of financial outcomes. Homeowners who understand this begin viewing shorter-term refinancing not as a burden but as a powerful wealth acceleration strategy.

Every extra dollar directed toward principal today reduces future interest tomorrow. Every shortened year removes financial obligations from the future. Every accelerated payment increases ownership and flexibility.

Mortgage freedom rarely happens accidentally. It is usually the result of intentional decisions repeated consistently over time.

Refinancing into a shorter-term mortgage is one of the most powerful of those decisions.

Refinancing Into a Shorter Loan Term

Let's look at a realistic example of how refinancing into a shorter loan term can create massive long-term interest savings and accelerate financial freedom.

Current Mortgage Situation

A homeowner currently has:

- Remaining Mortgage Balance: $500,000
- Current Interest Rate: 7.25%
- Remaining Loan Term: 27 Years

Current Monthly Principal & Interest Payment

Approximately:

$3,544 monthly

Option 1: Keep Existing Mortgage

If the homeowner keeps the current mortgage for the remaining 27 years:

Total Future Payments

$3{,}544 \times 324 = 1{,}148{,}256$

Total future payments:

$1,148,256

Total Future Interest

Total future payments:

$1,148,256

Minus remaining balance:

$500,000

Future Interest Cost

$1{,}148{,}256 - 500{,}000 = 648{,}256$

Approximate future interest:

$648,256

Option 2: Refinance Into a 15-Year Mortgage

The homeowner refinances strategically.

New Loan Structure

- New Loan Amount: $500,000
- New Interest Rate: 5.50%
- New Loan Term: 15 Years

New Monthly Principal & Interest Payment

Approximately:

$4,085 monthly

Payment Difference

New payment:

$4,085

Old payment:

$3,544

Monthly Increase

4,085−3,544=541

Monthly payment increase:

$541

Total Future Payments on New 15-Year Loan

4,085×180=735,300

Total future payments:

$735,300

Total Future Interest on New Loan

Total payments:

$735,300

Minus mortgage balance:

$500,000

Future Interest Cost

735,300−500,000=235,300

Approximate future interest:

$235,300

Total Interest Savings

Old mortgage future interest:

$648,256

New refinance future interest:

$235,300

Total Interest Saved

648,256−235,300=412,956

Approximate total interest savings:

$412,956

Time Saved

Original remaining timeline:

27 years

New timeline:

15 years

Years Eliminated

27−15=1227 - 15 = 1227−15=12

Mortgage paid off:

12 years earlier

Long-Term Financial Impact

By increasing the payment only:

$541 monthly

the homeowner:

- Saves over $400,000 in future interest
- Eliminates 12 years of mortgage payments
- Builds equity dramatically faster
- Increases long-term financial flexibility
- Potentially enters retirement mortgage-free

Optional Investment Scenario

Suppose after paying off the mortgage 12 years early, the homeowner invests the old mortgage payment instead.

Old mortgage payment:

$4,085 monthly

If invested monthly for 12 additional years at a hypothetical 7% annual return:

Approximate future investment value:

Over $1,000,000+

This demonstrates one of the most powerful concepts in personal finance:

Eliminating debt earlier creates future cash flow that can later build enormous wealth.

Emotional and Psychological Value

The math alone is powerful.

But the psychological benefits can be equally important:

- Reduced stress
- Increased security
- Greater career flexibility
- Stronger retirement readiness
- Freedom from long-term debt obligations

Many homeowners discover that shorter-term refinancing changes not only their mortgage balance but also their entire mindset about money, discipline, and long-term wealth creation.

Key Lesson

This example demonstrates that refinancing into a shorter-term mortgage is not simply about paying slightly more monthly.

It is about:

- Reducing massive future interest costs
- Reclaiming years of financial freedom
- Accelerating ownership
- Increasing long-term wealth potential

The homeowners who understand this principle often transform their financial futures permanently through one intentional refinance decision.

Chapter 9

Refinancing Strategically During Different Interest Rate Environments

One of the most important skills homeowners can develop is understanding how to refinance strategically during changing interest rate environments. Interest rates influence nearly every aspect of mortgage financing, from monthly payments and long-term interest costs to investment opportunities and overall financial flexibility. Yet many borrowers approach refinancing emotionally rather than strategically. They either panic when rates rise or become overly aggressive when rates fall, often making decisions without fully understanding the broader financial picture.

The reality is that every interest rate environment creates both opportunities and challenges. Low-rate environments may create powerful refinancing opportunities that dramatically improve mortgage efficiency. Rising-rate environments may require more selective strategies focused on preserving flexibility, reducing risk, or restructuring debt differently. Homeowners who understand how to adapt strategically to changing market conditions often place themselves in much stronger financial positions than those who simply react emotionally to headlines or market trends. To understand refinance timing properly, homeowners must first understand what drives mortgage rates. Mortgage interest rates are influenced by many factors including inflation, Federal Reserve policy, bond markets, economic growth, employment conditions, consumer spending, and investor confidence. Rates fluctuate constantly because financial markets continuously react to changing economic conditions and future expectations.

Inflation is one of the biggest drivers of interest rates. When inflation rises aggressively, lenders generally demand higher interest rates because future dollars lose purchasing power over time. Higher inflation increases lender risk because the money repaid years later may be worth less in real terms. In contrast, lower inflation environments often support lower mortgage rates because financial stability improves and lending risk declines.

Economic uncertainty also affects rates significantly. During recessions or periods of financial instability, governments and central banks may lower interest rates to stimulate borrowing, spending, and investment. Conversely, during periods of strong economic growth or overheating markets, rates may rise to control inflation and moderate economic activity.

Homeowners often make the mistake of viewing interest rates too simplistically. Many assume refinancing only makes sense when rates decline dramatically. While lower rates certainly create powerful opportunities, strategic refinancing decisions involve much more than rate comparisons alone. Loan structure, remaining loan term, mortgage insurance, cash flow goals, debt consolidation, investment opportunities, and long-term financial planning all matter as well.

For example, a homeowner may benefit from refinancing into a shorter-term loan even if rates only decline modestly because accelerated principal reduction dramatically lowers total interest costs. Another borrower may refinance to eliminate mortgage insurance or consolidate high-interest debt despite rates remaining relatively stable. The refinance strategy should always align with the homeowner's overall financial objectives rather than focusing exclusively on rate movements.

Low-interest-rate environments create some of the most obvious refinancing opportunities. When rates decline substantially below existing mortgage rates, homeowners may lower monthly payments, reduce long-term interest expenses, shorten loan terms, or improve cash flow significantly. Many financially disciplined homeowners use these periods strategically to accelerate wealth building and debt reduction.

One powerful strategy during low-rate environments involves refinancing into shorter loan terms while keeping payments manageable. Lower rates offset some of the payment increase associated with shorter amortization schedules, allowing borrowers to eliminate debt dramatically faster without extreme monthly increases.

For example, a homeowner refinancing from a seven-percent thirty-year mortgage into a five-percent fifteen-year loan may save hundreds of thousands of dollars in interest while shortening the repayment timeline substantially. This type of strategic refinance can permanently improve long-term financial positioning.

Low-rate environments may also create opportunities for cash-out refinancing used productively. Borrowing against home equity at lower mortgage rates may provide relatively inexpensive capital for investments, business growth, rental property acquisitions, or high-interest debt elimination. However, homeowners must remain disciplined because low rates can also encourage excessive borrowing and overleveraging.

Many people become financially reckless during low-rate environments because borrowing feels cheap. They refinance repeatedly, increase debt excessively, or fund lifestyle inflation instead of productive investments. Financial discipline matters more than interest rates alone. Low borrowing costs do not eliminate risk.

Rising-rate environments create different strategic considerations. Many homeowners assume refinancing becomes impossible or pointless when rates rise. This is not always true. Even during rising-rate periods, refinancing may still improve financial outcomes depending on the borrower's current situation.

For example, a homeowner with significant high-interest credit card debt may still benefit from refinancing into a slightly higher mortgage rate if the refinance dramatically lowers overall interest costs across all debts combined. Another borrower may refinance an adjustable-rate mortgage into a fixed-rate structure for long-term stability despite higher current rates.

Fixed-rate stability becomes especially valuable during volatile interest rate environments. Homeowners carrying adjustable-rate mortgages may face payment uncertainty if rates continue rising aggressively. Refinancing into fixed-rate loans may provide predictability and protection even if rates are higher than previous market lows.

Psychology plays a massive role in refinance timing decisions. Many borrowers become paralyzed waiting for the "perfect" interest rate. They delay refinancing repeatedly hoping rates will fall slightly further, only to miss opportunities entirely when rates rise unexpectedly. Others rush into refinances impulsively because of fear or market hype without analyzing long-term implications carefully.

The goal should not necessarily be finding the absolute lowest possible rate. Instead, homeowners should focus on whether refinancing meaningfully improves their financial position based on their goals, timeline, and overall strategy.

Break-even analysis becomes extremely important when evaluating refinance timing. Refinancing involves closing costs including lender fees, appraisal charges, title expenses, escrow adjustments, and prepaid items. Borrowers should calculate how long monthly savings or financial improvements will take to exceed these upfront costs.

For example, if refinancing costs $7,000 but reduces expenses by $500 monthly, the break-even point occurs after approximately fourteen months. If the homeowner plans to keep the property substantially longer than that, the refinance may still create major long-term value.

Homeowners should also consider opportunity cost during different rate environments. Opportunity cost refers to what is sacrificed by choosing one financial option over another. For example, aggressively paying down a very low fixed-rate mortgage during inflationary environments may produce less long-term wealth than investing excess cash elsewhere depending on market conditions and investment returns.

However, many homeowners still prioritize mortgage reduction because they value security, simplicity, and guaranteed debt elimination more highly than uncertain investment outcomes. Neither perspective is universally correct. The best strategy depends on individual goals, risk tolerance, and financial philosophy.

Cash flow management becomes even more important during uncertain economic conditions. Rising rates often increase pressure across the economy because borrowing costs rise for consumers and businesses alike. Homeowners with strong cash flow flexibility generally handle economic uncertainty far better than those stretched excessively thin.

This is why some borrowers refinance into longer terms strategically even when rates remain stable or rise modestly. Lower required payments may strengthen liquidity and financial resilience during uncertain times. Others choose shorter terms because they prioritize eliminating debt aggressively before rates rise further. Again, intentionality matters most. Property appreciation cycles also influence refinancing opportunities. During strong real estate markets, homeowners may build equity rapidly through appreciation alone. This improved equity position may create refinance eligibility for lower rates, mortgage insurance elimination, or cash-out opportunities even if broader rate environments become less favorable.

Conversely, declining property values may limit refinance options because loan-to-value ratios worsen. Homeowners should therefore avoid relying entirely on appreciation assumptions when planning refinance strategies.

Another important consideration involves refinancing frequency. Some homeowners refinance repeatedly whenever rates decline slightly. While occasional strategic refinancing can create substantial benefits, excessive refinancing may generate unnecessary costs and continually restart amortization schedules negatively.

Strategic borrowers evaluate whether each refinance creates meaningful long-term improvement rather than chasing minor short-term savings repeatedly.

Credit quality also affects refinance opportunities significantly across all rate environments. Borrowers with strong credit profiles generally qualify for the best available rates and loan structures. Improving credit scores before refinancing may therefore create meaningful long-term savings even if broader market rates remain unchanged.

Some homeowners become discouraged when rates rise because they assume they "missed their chance." This mindset can become financially harmful. Even during higher-rate environments, homeowners may still improve financial positioning through term adjustments, debt consolidation, mortgage insurance removal, or restructuring strategies.

Financial success rarely comes from perfectly timing markets. It usually comes from consistent, intentional decision-making over time.

One of the most important principles homeowners should understand is that mortgage management is not passive. Too many borrowers obtain mortgages and then ignore them for decades regardless of changing economic conditions or personal financial growth. Financially sophisticated individuals actively monitor rates, evaluate opportunities, improve loan structures, and adjust strategies as conditions evolve.

Refinancing is not simply about reacting to markets. It is about proactively managing debt as part of a larger financial system designed to support long-term goals.

Ultimately, every interest rate environment creates different opportunities. Low-rate periods may favor aggressive refinancing and debt acceleration. Rising-rate periods may emphasize stability, liquidity, and strategic restructuring. The key is understanding how to adapt intelligently rather than emotionally.

Mortgage rates will always fluctuate over time. Homeowners cannot control the market itself, but they can control how they respond to it. Those responses shape long-term financial outcomes dramatically.

The homeowners who build lasting wealth are often not those who perfectly predict interest rate movements. They are the ones who consistently make thoughtful, disciplined decisions aligned with their broader financial goals regardless of market conditions.

Strategic refinancing is not about chasing headlines.

It is about building long-term financial freedom intentionally through changing economic environments.

Refinancing in Different Interest Rate Environments

Let's compare how refinancing strategies may differ depending on changing market conditions.

Scenario 1: Low Interest Rate Environment

Original Mortgage

A homeowner currently has:

- Mortgage Balance: $450,000
- Current Interest Rate: 7.25%
- Remaining Loan Term: 28 Years

Current Monthly Principal & Interest Payment

Approximately:

$3,203 monthly

Low-Rate Market Opportunity

Mortgage rates fall significantly.

The homeowner refinances into:

- New Interest Rate: 5.00%
- New Loan Term: 20 Years

New Monthly Payment

Approximately:

$2,970 monthly

Monthly Savings

Old payment:

$3,203

New payment:

$2,970

Monthly Savings

3,203−2,970=233

Monthly savings:

$233

Timeline Improvement

Original remaining term:

28 years

New term:

20 years

Years Eliminated

28−20=8

Mortgage paid off:

8 years earlier

Interest Savings

Existing Mortgage Future Payments

3,203×336=1,076,208

Total future payments:

$1,076,208

Minus mortgage balance:

$450,000

Future Interest Cost

1,076,208−450,000=626,208

Approximate future interest:

$626,208

New Refinance Future Payments

2,970×240=712,800

Total future payments:

$712,800

Minus mortgage balance:

$450,000

Future Interest Cost

712,800−450,000=262,800

Approximate future interest:

$262,800

Total Interest Saved

626,208−262,800=363,408

Approximate interest savings:

$363,408

Scenario 2: Rising Interest Rate Environment

Now imagine rates rise instead of fall.

The homeowner currently has:

- Adjustable-rate mortgage starting at 4.25%
- Remaining balance: $450,000

The adjustable rate is expected to rise to approximately 7.50% over the next adjustment period.

Current payment:

$2,213 monthly

Projected adjusted payment:

Approximately:

$3,147 monthly

Strategic Refinance for Stability

The homeowner refinances into:

- Fixed interest rate: 6.25%
- New loan term: 25 Years

New Fixed Monthly Payment

Approximately:

$2,958 monthly

Why This Still Helps

Although the new fixed payment is higher than the original adjustable payment, it protects the homeowner from future uncertainty and rising rates.

Instead of risking future increases beyond 7.50%, the borrower locks in stability and predictability.

Payment Comparison

Projected adjustable payment:

$3,147

New fixed payment:

$2,958

Monthly Savings Compared to Future Adjustment

$3{,}147 - 2{,}958 = 189$

Monthly savings:

$189

plus long-term payment stability.

Debt Consolidation Example During Rising Rates

Suppose the homeowner also has:

- Credit card debt: $35,000 at 23% interest

Annual interest on credit cards:

$35{,}000 \times 0.23 = 8{,}050$

Annual credit card interest:

$8,050

By consolidating this debt into the refinance at 6.25%:

Approximate annual interest:

$35{,}000 \times 0.0625 = 2{,}187.50$

Approximate annual interest:

$2,187.50

Annual Interest Savings

8,050−2,187.5=5,862.50

Approximate yearly savings:

$5,862.50

Key Lesson

This example demonstrates that refinancing strategies should adapt to different market environments.

In Low-Rate Environments:

- Homeowners may aggressively shorten loan terms
- Massive interest savings become possible
- Debt acceleration becomes highly efficient

In Rising-Rate Environments:

- Stability and fixed payments become valuable
- Debt restructuring may still improve cash flow
- High-interest debt consolidation may remain extremely beneficial

The most successful homeowners are not necessarily those who predict markets perfectly.

They are the ones who understand how to respond strategically to changing conditions while staying focused on long-term financial freedom.

Chapter 10

The Complete Mortgage Refinancing Strategy for Financial Freedom

At this stage in the series, it should be clear that mortgage refinancing is not a single isolated decision. It is a long-term financial strategy that evolves over time and interacts with interest rates, loan terms, equity growth, income changes, debt structures, and broader wealth-building goals. The most financially successful homeowners do not refinance randomly or emotionally. Instead, they follow a structured approach that allows them to consistently improve their financial position over decades.

The complete mortgage refinancing strategy is about combining everything learned in previous chapters into a unified system. It is not just about lowering payments, reducing interest rates, or cashing out equity. It is about using refinancing as a dynamic financial tool that adapts to life changes and accelerates long-term financial freedom.

Most homeowners approach refinancing reactively. They wait until interest rates drop, until financial stress increases, or until a lender reaches out with an offer. This reactive approach often leads to missed opportunities or inefficient financial decisions. A strategic borrower, however, takes a proactive approach. They continuously evaluate whether their current mortgage structure is aligned with their goals and adjust it when meaningful improvements are available.

A complete refinancing strategy begins with clarity of purpose. Every refinance should serve a specific financial objective. That objective may be reducing total interest paid, shortening the loan term, eliminating mortgage insurance, consolidating high-interest debt, increasing cash flow, accessing equity for investment purposes, or improving long-term financial stability. Without a clear objective, refinancing becomes guesswork rather than strategy.

The second step in a complete strategy is understanding the trade-offs involved in every refinance decision. There is no such thing as a free refinance. Every decision involves costs, whether in the form of closing expenses, extended loan terms, increased debt balances, or long-term interest trade-offs. A strategic borrower evaluates whether the long-term financial benefits outweigh the short-term costs.

For example, lowering a monthly payment may feel beneficial immediately, but if it significantly extends the loan term, the borrower may end up paying far more in total interest over time. Conversely, increasing a payment slightly to shorten the loan term may feel uncomfortable initially but could save hundreds of thousands of dollars in the long run. Strategic refinancing requires balancing short-term comfort with long-term efficiency.

Another core principle is timing flexibility. A complete mortgage strategy does not rely on perfect timing of interest rates. Instead, it focuses on capturing meaningful opportunities when they arise. Many homeowners delay refinancing while waiting for rates to drop slightly further, only to miss opportunities entirely when market conditions shift. A strategic borrower understands that refinancing should be based on overall financial improvement rather than chasing the absolute lowest possible rate.

Loan structure optimization is another critical component. The best refinance decisions often involve more than just interest rate adjustments. Loan term selection, amortization structure, payment flexibility, and principal reduction strategies all play major roles in long-term financial outcomes. A borrower who understands how to align loan structure with income stability, cash flow needs, and long-term goals will consistently outperform borrowers who focus only on monthly payment changes. Equity utilization also plays a key role in a complete strategy. Home equity is one of the largest financial assets many households possess, yet it is often underutilized or misunderstood. Strategic refinancing allows homeowners to unlock equity when it creates productive financial outcomes, such as eliminating high-interest debt, funding income-producing investments, or strengthening overall liquidity. However, equity should never be extracted without a clear plan for value creation.

Cash flow management is equally important. A refinance should improve the overall cash flow position of the household either directly or indirectly. Direct improvements come from lower monthly payments or eliminated expenses such as mortgage insurance. Indirect improvements come from restructuring debt in a way that frees up capital for investing, saving, or accelerating mortgage payoff. Cash flow is the foundation of financial flexibility, and refinancing should strengthen it whenever possible.

A complete mortgage strategy also considers risk management. Debt is not inherently bad, but excessive or poorly structured debt increases financial vulnerability. A well-designed refinance strategy reduces unnecessary risk exposure by stabilizing payments, eliminating high-interest obligations, and improving liquidity. This creates resilience during economic downturns, job changes, or unexpected financial disruptions. One of the most overlooked elements of refinancing strategy is behavioral discipline. Even the most mathematically optimal refinance structure will fail if the borrower does not maintain disciplined financial behavior afterward. For example, consolidating credit card debt through a refinance only creates long-term benefit if the borrower avoids rebuilding that debt again. Without behavior change, refinancing simply resets the cycle rather than breaking it.

A successful long-term strategy also incorporates periodic financial reviews. Mortgage structures should not remain static for decades. As income increases, property values change, interest rates fluctuate, and financial goals evolve, homeowners should periodically reassess whether their mortgage structure is still optimal. This does not mean refinancing constantly, but rather staying aware of opportunities for meaningful improvement.

Another key principle is integration with broader financial planning. A mortgage should never exist in isolation from retirement planning, investment strategy, tax planning, business development, or savings goals. A refinance that improves mortgage efficiency but harms investment capacity may not be optimal. Similarly, a refinance that increases cash flow while enabling stronger long-term investments may significantly improve overall financial outcomes. Tax considerations may also influence refinance decisions depending on jurisdiction and financial structure. Mortgage interest deductions, investment property strategies, and business-related refinancing can all impact after-tax outcomes. Strategic borrowers evaluate both pre-tax and after-tax implications when making decisions.

Psychological alignment is another important factor. Financial strategies must align with personal values and lifestyle preferences. Some homeowners prioritize debt freedom above all else. Others prioritize liquidity and investment growth. Others value stability and predictability. A successful refinancing strategy respects these preferences while still optimizing financial outcomes.

Ultimately, the complete mortgage refinancing strategy is about control. It is about shifting from a passive borrower mindset to an active financial management mindset. Instead of allowing the mortgage to dictate financial progress over thirty years, homeowners learn to actively shape the mortgage structure over time to support evolving goals.

Financial freedom does not come from a single refinance. It comes from a series of intentional decisions made consistently over time. Each refinance should represent progress toward a broader objective rather than an isolated transaction. When viewed this way, refinancing becomes a powerful long-term wealth-building tool rather than just a temporary financial adjustment.

The homeowners who achieve the greatest financial success are those who understand that their mortgage is not fixed permanently. It is flexible. It can be optimized, restructured, accelerated, and improved. The key is awareness combined with disciplined execution.

A complete refinancing strategy recognizes that financial freedom is not a single moment. It is a process. It is built through small, strategic improvements that compound over years and decades. Lower interest rates, shorter loan terms, eliminated insurance, reduced high-interest debt, optimized cash flow, and intelligent equity usage all contribute to that process.

When combined correctly, these elements transform the mortgage from a long-term financial burden into a strategic wealth-building instrument. Instead of working against the homeowner, the mortgage begins working with them.

The ultimate goal is not just to own a home. The goal is to own the home efficiently, with minimal unnecessary interest costs, maximum financial flexibility, and a clear path toward debt freedom and long-term wealth creation.

A complete mortgage refinancing strategy makes that goal

achievable.

Real-Life Math Example: Full Strategic Refinancing Plan in Action

Let's combine multiple refinancing strategies into one realistic scenario to show how a complete plan can transform a homeowner's financial future.

Initial Situation

A homeowner currently has:

Primary Mortgage

- Balance: $420,000
- Interest Rate: 7.00%
- Remaining Term: 26 Years
- Monthly Payment: $2,793

Additional Debts

- Credit Cards: $25,000 at 22% interest
- Auto Loan: $18,000 at 9% interest

Total Monthly Debt Payments

Mortgage: $2,793 Credit Cards: $700 Auto Loan: $410

Total Monthly Outflow

2,793+700+410=3,903

Total monthly debt payments:

$3,903

Strategic Refinancing Plan

The homeowner executes a comprehensive refinance strategy:

Step 1: Cash-Out Refinance

New mortgage includes debt consolidation and restructuring:

- New Loan Amount: $470,000
- New Interest Rate: 5.75%
- New Term: 20 Years

Funds used:

- Pay off credit cards: $25,000
- Pay off auto loan: $18,000

- Closing costs: $7,000

Step 2: New Mortgage Payment

Approximate new monthly payment:

$3,289

Step 3: Monthly Cash Flow Comparison

Old total monthly payments:

$3,903

New mortgage payment:

$3,289

Monthly Savings

$3{,}903 - 3{,}289 = 614$

Monthly improvement:

$614

Step 4: Annual Cash Flow Improvement

$614 \times 12 = 7{,}368$

Annual improvement:

$7,368

Step 5: Interest Rate Savings on Eliminated Debt

Credit Card Interest Saved

$25{,}000 \times 0.22 = 5{,}500$

Credit card interest eliminated:

$5,500/year

Auto Loan Interest Saved

$18{,}000 \times 0.09 = 1{,}620$

Auto loan interest eliminated:

$1,620/year

Step 6: Total Interest Savings

$5{,}500 + 1{,}620 = 7{,}120$

Total annual interest savings:

$7,120

Step 7: Combined Financial Impact

Cash flow improvement:

$7,368/year

Interest savings:

$7,120/year

Total Annual Financial Improvement

7,368+7,120=14,488

Total annual benefit:

$14,488

Step 8: Accelerated Mortgage Payoff Strategy

If the homeowner applies the $614 monthly savings toward principal:

614×12=7,368

Additional annual principal reduction:

$7,368

Over 10 years:

7,368×10=73,6807,368 \times 10 = 73,6807,368×10=73,680

Extra principal reduction:

$73,680

Final Outcome

Through one strategic refinance:

- High-interest debt eliminated
- Monthly payments reduced
- Cash flow improved by $614/month
- Over $14,000/year in combined financial benefit
- Mortgage payoff accelerated significantly
- Long-term wealth trajectory improved

Key Lesson

This example demonstrates how a complete refinancing strategy is not about a single change, but about combining multiple advantages:

- Debt consolidation
- Interest rate reduction
- Loan term optimization
- Cash flow improvement
- Principal acceleration

When used together, refinancing becomes a full financial restructuring system that can dramatically accelerate wealth building and financial freedom.

Final Tips and Suggestions for Mortgage Freedom

Reaching mortgage freedom is not the result of a single strategy, one refinance, or a perfect interest rate. It is the outcome of consistent financial decisions made over time with clarity, discipline, and intention. Throughout this series, you have seen how refinancing, loan term selection, interest rate optimization, cash flow management, and debt structuring all interact to shape the long-term cost of homeownership. The final step is bringing everything together into a practical mindset and action framework that allows you to move from learning to execution.

The most important concept to understand is that mortgage freedom is a process, not an event. Many homeowners think in terms of "paying off the house someday," but financially successful individuals think in terms of systems. They do not wait passively for time to pass. They actively engineer their mortgage outcome through structured decisions. Every payment, refinance, and allocation of extra cash either accelerates or delays freedom. There is no neutral position.

One of the most powerful habits you can develop is regularly reviewing your mortgage. Most people obtain a mortgage and then ignore it for years. They accept the original terms as permanent even when their financial situation improves significantly. A better approach is to evaluate your mortgage at least once a year. Ask simple but powerful questions: Has my interest rate become outdated compared to the market? Has my equity position improved enough to eliminate mortgage insurance? Has my income increased enough to support a shorter loan term? Has my debt structure changed in a way that justifies refinancing?

Small improvements over time can create massive long-term results. Even a one percent reduction in interest rate or a five-year reduction in loan term can translate into tens or hundreds of thousands of dollars saved over the life of a mortgage. The key is not waiting for perfect conditions but acting when meaningful improvement is available.

Another essential tip is understanding the difference between affordability and efficiency. Many homeowners focus only on whether they can afford a monthly payment. While affordability is important, efficiency determines long-term wealth outcomes. A lower payment that extends debt for decades may feel comfortable but can be extremely expensive over time. A slightly higher payment that shortens the loan term or reduces interest can create significantly greater financial freedom in the long run. The goal is not just to survive monthly payments but to optimize the total cost of borrowing. Cash flow discipline is one of the strongest predictors of mortgage freedom success. When income increases, many people immediately expand their lifestyle. This is known as lifestyle inflation. While improving quality of life is natural, uncontrolled lifestyle expansion often prevents financial progress. A more strategic approach is to assign purpose to additional income. When you receive raises, bonuses, commissions, or unexpected income, decide in advance what percentage will go toward mortgage acceleration, savings, investments, or debt reduction. Without intentional allocation, money tends to disappear into spending habits without creating long-term value.

Another important principle is consistency in extra payments. Even small additional principal payments can have a significant impact over time because they reduce the loan balance on which interest is calculated. When interest is reduced, future payments become more effective. Many homeowners underestimate how powerful consistent extra payments can be. An additional $200 to $500 per month applied directly to principal can shorten a mortgage by years and save substantial interest over time.

However, consistency matters more than intensity. One large payment followed by years of inactivity is less powerful than steady, disciplined contributions over time. Mortgage freedom is built through repetition, not occasional effort. It is also important to maintain emergency reserves while pursuing mortgage payoff strategies. One of the biggest financial mistakes homeowners make is becoming overly aggressive with debt reduction while neglecting liquidity. Financial stability requires balance. Ideally, you should have sufficient emergency savings to cover unexpected expenses such as job changes, medical bills, or home repairs. Without reserves, you may be forced to rely on high-interest debt again, which reverses progress. A strong mortgage strategy always includes protection against financial shocks.

Refinancing should be viewed as a tool, not a goal. Many homeowners focus on refinancing repeatedly without a clear long-term plan. Each refinance should serve a specific purpose such as reducing interest, shortening the loan term, eliminating mortgage insurance, consolidating debt, or improving cash flow. If a refinance does not clearly improve your financial position, it may not be necessary. The best refinances are intentional, not habitual.

Equity awareness is another key factor in mortgage freedom. Many homeowners do not regularly track how much equity they have built in their homes. Equity represents financial progress and potential flexibility. As equity increases, opportunities expand. You may qualify for better refinancing options, eliminate mortgage insurance, or even restructure debt more efficiently. Monitoring equity allows you to make informed decisions rather than guessing your financial position.

It is also important to think long-term about retirement. One of the most effective ways to improve retirement readiness is to eliminate housing payments before retirement begins. A mortgage-free retirement significantly reduces financial pressure and increases flexibility. Instead of relying on fixed retirement income to cover housing costs, homeowners without mortgages can allocate resources toward healthcare, travel, investments, or legacy planning. Mortgage freedom is often one of the strongest foundations of retirement security.

Another important mindset shift involves understanding that debt is not just a burden, but a system that can be optimized. Many people view mortgages emotionally, as something stressful to eliminate as quickly as possible. While emotional relief is important, strategic thinking creates better long-term outcomes. In some cases, maintaining a low-interest mortgage while investing excess cash may be beneficial. In other cases, aggressive payoff may be the best option. The correct strategy depends on your goals, risk tolerance, and financial structure.

Education remains one of the most powerful tools in achieving mortgage freedom. The more you understand how amortization works, how interest accumulates, how refinancing structures operate, and how loan terms affect total cost, the more control you gain over your financial future. Financial literacy turns confusion into clarity and transforms reactive decisions into strategic ones.

Avoiding unnecessary debt is equally important. While mortgages are often considered "good debt" compared to consumer debt, every loan still represents an obligation. Reducing unnecessary borrowing allows more income to flow toward wealth-building activities rather than interest payments. The fewer financial obligations you carry, the faster you can achieve freedom.

Patience also plays a critical role. Mortgage freedom is rarely achieved overnight. It is a long-term process that rewards consistency more than speed. Many homeowners become discouraged when progress feels slow in the early years. However, financial momentum builds over time. As balances decrease and interest compounds less aggressively, progress accelerates. The later stages of mortgage payoff often feel significantly faster than the early years.

One of the most powerful final suggestions is to create a clear mortgage freedom target. Instead of simply making payments without direction, define a specific payoff timeline or goal. Whether it is ten years, fifteen years, or twenty years, having a target creates focus and accountability. Goals transform abstract financial behavior into measurable progress.

Finally, remember that mortgage freedom is not just about eliminating debt. It is about creating options. It is about gaining control over your time, reducing financial stress, increasing investment capacity, and building long-term security. A paid-off mortgage does not just remove a payment; it unlocks financial flexibility that can reshape your entire lifestyle.

The homeowners who succeed in achieving mortgage freedom are not necessarily those with the highest incomes. They are the ones who make intentional decisions consistently over time. They understand the impact of interest, the value of equity, the importance of discipline, and the power of strategic refinancing. Most importantly, they stay focused on the long-term outcome even when short-term distractions appear.

If you apply the principles from this series consistently, mortgage freedom becomes not just possible, but highly achievable. It is the result of systems, not luck. It is the result of structure, not chance. And it is the result of commitment, not complexity.

Every mortgage payment is a choice. Every refinance is a decision. Every extra dollar applied toward principal is a step forward. Over time, those steps compound into something powerful: financial independence.

The path to mortgage freedom is clear. The only question that remains is how intentionally you choose to walk it.

www.ingramcontent.com/pod-product-compliance
Ingram Content Group UK Ltd.
Pitfield, Milton Keynes, MK11 3LW, UK
UKHW010011031026
15589UKWH00008B/1598

9 798256 007492